LAW FOR IT PROFESSIONALS

Paul Brennan
General Counsel, FAST

© Paul Brennan 2003

Published by
emis professional publishing ltd
31–33 Stonehills House
Welwyn Garden City
Hertfordshire
AL8 6PU

ISBN 1 85811 322 9

Typeset by Jane Conway

Cover design by Jane Conway
Cover photography by Jon Adams

Illustrations by Martha Hardy (Beehive Illustration)
Concepts © Paul Brennan

Printed in Great Britain by Antony Rowe

Dedicated to

My wife Diane and my children Edward, Alice, Paddy and Kathleen

CONTENTS

FOREWORD

FAST protect the rights of software owners and also provides advice and guidance to end users.

We are aware that the greatest problem both sides have is ensuring compliance with the law. The risk of non-compliance is often overlooked by the end user of software who increasingly relies upon the support of their IT team for whom compliance, now driven by a plethora of laws, is a real headache.

Paul Brennan's book meets a real need to cut through the apparent complexity of the situation that these IT Professionals face. Born out of the advice that FAST members have sought, it provides answers to real questions asked by real people.

For FAST members, trained through the FAST program, it will provide a real boon as a ready reference. For many non-FAST members it will be a revelation – highlighting legal obligations that were previously dismissed as irrelevant and providing simple answers to what seemed intractable issues.

Better still, the book is fun to read. Paul's cartoons and light touch ensure that more than any other law book on IT, I can recommend it.

Geoffrey Webster
CEO
FAST
Aug, 2003

PREFACE

This book is intended to give IT Professionals the bottom line. To list all the legal topics that they should be aware of in one place and then to provide basic information on each of the topics. This should give the IT Professional what he needs to know to be professional without burdening him with legal detail. I try to alert IT Professionals to legal issues where if they get it wrong they may be in big trouble. In these cases they must get legal help and that means them or their company instructing a lawyer with all the accompanying worry of expense.

It is important for the IT Professional to use the right legal terminology. Referring to patents when you mean copyright will not impress employers. In today's climate they want someone who sounds credible looking after their IT environment: there is often too much money at stake to take a chance on someone who does not appear to be professional.

I have based this book on my dealings with some of the 3,000 highly professional IT Managers from companies large and small participating in the FAST program. My legal team noted that there were questions that were asked with great regularity. There appeared to be about twenty main areas of the law which were of interest to these IT Managers. The twenty areas of law are licensing, pornography, data protection, RIPA, confidentiality agreements, restrictive covenants, outsourcing, mergers and acquisitions, litigation, policies, internet investigations, directors' liability, copyright, vicarious liability, defamation, human rights, distance selling, websites, electronic signatures and contracts (in particular computer services contracts).

The book is divided into four parts. It first explains the law about which IT Professionals should be aware. Many of the IT Professional's problems stem from the misuse of systems by employees and consultants (wouldn't life be so much easier without them). This is the subject of Part Two. Part Three applies this legal know-how to the challenges in practice: divided into high risk and routine issues. It also deals with routine issues such as licensing.

Part Four deals with the legal emergencies which confront the IT Professional for example gathering evidence when the company is suing or being sued.

The FAST membership also includes over 150 companies in the Software Industry. Software publishers, resellers, distributors, IT/IP lawyers and various consultants. People in these companies not only needed to understand the law applying to the protection of their products but also the law which concerned the IT Manager. Frequently the Software Industry would use their knowledge of the law of concern to the IT Manager as a route to market.

It has been necessary to identify the main legislation however section numbers and details of regulations have been kept to a minimum. I have met many people who are very good on the section numbers and know the names of the acts but do not know what they really do. The intention in this book is for the reader to painlessly gain an understanding of the law.

I have tried to keep the law simple. I have ignored the many ifs, buts and exceptions which are the life blood of the law in order to give the reader a straightforward understandable explanation. Let all lawyers and experts in the many fields covered in this book excuse me for the many generalisations.

Where I have needed to use a gender to describe a person I have consistently used "he" rather than "her". There are many highly capable female IT Professionals I hope they understand that it was just easier to use "he".

I sincerely hope that IT Professional will enjoy reading this book. I realise that many joined the IT Industry with a passion for computers. They did not expect to be confronted by such a variety of complex legal issues in this fast moving area of the law. However an understanding of IT law is vital to today's IT Professional.

Paul Brennan

PART 1
THE LAW

COPYRIGHT!

CHAPTER 1
INTELLECTUAL PROPERTY RIGHTS
IN BRIEF

The *Financial Times* reported in 2002 that "Intellectual Property is today's competitive weapon.... Identifying, registering and protecting Intellectual Property Rights has emerged as one of the key drivers of business competitiveness in the 21st century."

Most businessmen lack a sufficient understanding of Intellectual Property Rights (IPR).

IPR is property. In law, land is called "real property" however IPR is not real and cannot be touched. The French say that IPR is the product of the mind.

There are basically five types of IPR. These are copyright, designs, patents, databases and trademarks. These rights are mainly contained in two Acts of Parliament. The first in the Copyright, Designs and Patent Act 1988; databases were more recently added to this Act. Trademarks have their own Act called the Trademarks Act 1994.

IPRs protect information. In a modern society information has great value. It is very often simply information that we buy and sell.

If anybody could for instance, freely copy software, a film or music at any time, or manufacture drugs at will then the film, music and drug industries would lose billions. Add to this corporations which rely on IPR to protect their big brands in products such as drinks, clothing and fast food etc. and you will appreciate there are many powerful industries relying on IPR to protect their investments. Governments are aware that without strong IPR jobs and revenue would be lost. Therefore the legal protection afforded to IPR is intended to be very strong.

Just before we examine the various IPRs a word of warning. The law protecting IPR is unusual.

1. Copyright

This is the most important IPR. It protects, among other things, software, books, film and music.

The concept of copyright started in the 15th Century with the advent of printing. Suddenly it was possible to make many copies of say a phamplet or a book. This right to copy needed to be controlled by the King, as he did not want mass distribution of literature. He was concerned that this new technology may be used to criticise him. Censorship was required. The King created an early version of a closed shop. He set up a Guild called the Stationers Company. Only Guild members were allowed to be publishers. Therefore, authors took their finished manuscript to a Guild member. The Guild member bought the manuscript from the author who had no further rights in the manuscript. The Guild member had "copyright" of the manuscript and then published it and kept all profits.

Interesting? Copyright can be fascinating. However I am compelled to tell you at this stage that any examination of copyright beyond a few pages and in some cases a few paragraphs makes the eyes of any normal person start to glaze over. If you do not believe me there are many books on copyright to support my theory. I suggest you try and pick one under 300 pages.

For those of you who have decided that you have insufficient time to make a detailed study of copyright then there are ten things that the IT professional should know about copyright.

1. Software is a copyright work and therefore protected by copyright. It is protected by copyright because the Copyright Designs and Patent Act 1988 says it is, not for any arcane legal reason. Remember IPRs have strong legal protection. This is

good news for the software publishers and bad news for anyone copying software.

2.   Some copyright works can claim multiple copyright protection. For instance, a game can have several different copyright works such as the music, the graphics, the literary work in the story and the software program itself. So if a producer of a game cannot establish his right to sue under one type of copyright then he will try to sue under another. For historic reasons the protection afforded to each of the different types of work are slightly different making copyright complicated.

3.   Copyright is about money. In the old days you wrote a book, collected small royalties and lived in a garret. Now you write a book then people must come to you to buy the right to merchandise, produce a film, perform a play, use the words with music as well as publish the book. There being more than one copyright attached to one software application may be a nuisance to learn and understand. However, in cash terms copyright is fantastic. It enables you to sell your work again and again. Therefore copyright is fiercely argued over and there are a lot of camps arguing for their piece of the pie.

4.   Copyright is international. International treaties driven by money concerns have in effect made copyright international. So write a computer program in the UK and you can enforce it if someone rips it off in Australia. Like everything in copyright there are exceptions, complications and expense.

5.   No registration required. Obtaining copyright protection is cheap, quick and easy. It applies as soon as you put the idea on paper or in code. For instance, take a piece of paper and scribble a quick 30-second doodle. Provided you have not copied anyone else, then that "work" is your copyright. No registration required or in this country possible. Isn't that neat?

6.   Ownership can be difficult to prove. There is a problem with copyright. Take your 30-second doodle. I assume that this will remain valueless. A company with a lousy computer program for sale will not be bothered by people trying to steal it. But what happens if you walk out on the street tomorrow and

people are wearing tee shirts bearing your doodle? The following day people are selling the tee shirts at tube stations and people are putting your doodle on posters which are appearing on wall after wall. On day three, your doodle becomes the new @ symbol for the internet, and email. After 10 days your doodle is more famous than the Che Guevara poster. Are they allowed to take your doodle and do this? Hell no, you have copyright. This may be an extreme example but software programs even simple ones can wing their way across corporations and the Internet. They are bought once and copied many times. So you have copyright but trying to enforce it in these circumstances is like shutting the stable door after the horse has bolted.

So if your doodle is worth stealing how do you try to control people ripping you off? The answer lies in the type of thing people say when they get caught.

Answer 1 (when/if caught) "This is not your doodle it's mine you have no right to stop me using it". That is why software developers embed their names in computer code to demonstrate to a judge that it is theirs. You should keep evidence of the initial design and call witnesses who knew that you drew it. If you are a new developer you can put your work into an envelope and send it to a trusted person like a solicitor. This will provide evidence that you created it and when.

Answer 2 (when/if caught): "But you let me use the doodle." Defendants who are caught red handed often say you gave them permission to use it. Sometimes this is by your actions. This "implied licence" is difficult to argue against. They will refer to conversations where you said go ahead and use it. They may have contributed to the work in some way e.g. a former employee or consultant.

Just as you did not expect that your doodle would be capable of making millions few people know which one of their copyright works will be a winner.

So it is best to start with the rule that no one uses your doodle without your permission. Something as short as the © symbol with your name and the year will alert any user that you are claiming copyright in the doodle. They need to come and ask for your permission. The consequences of not doing so are that copies of your doodles could be seized from unsuspecting purchasers. People dealing in your doodle could be sent to prison. When asked for your permission you would charge a fee for giving it. When you give this permission it is called a "licence" it does not sell the doodle but the right to use it. So too, a licence of a software program gives a right to use it. To be sure the licence had better say that the use of the doodle is limited to tee shirts. Then when another person comes along and wants to use it for swimsuits you can licence that right too. But what if the tee shirt business gets really hot and the licensee will make millions selling all over the world. Hopefully you have said in your licence that the right is limited to the UK. Then you can licence the right for each country. What if everyone in the UK wants a shirt with your doodle? Hopefully you have put a term in the licence document limiting the number of copies that the licensee can make so that you can sell him the right to manufacture more. People will start to say that your licences are too complicated but you do not know where your next doodle is coming from. These complicated licences are making you millions of £s. You decide to keep them and put up with the criticism.

The last thing people who design software want to do is to pay legal fees to prepare a licence. Often they just take a form of wording for a licence from a similar product. I put aside the fact that the copyright in the licence may belong to someone else. Some form of licence is better than none. But just like the doodle if you fail to limit the right geographically or the number of copies you may loose a lot of money. So really it is worth paying for a lawyer to design a licence just for your doodle. (Isn't it?)

However if your doodle is the valueless scribble that it seemed to be at the start you have nothing to worry about. But create something that has value and bandits will buzz around it like flies. At least consider a licence.

7. Who owns the copyright? If you created the work e.g. the doodle, then, you own it. However what happens if you are an employee and you create some software as part of your job? Or you are a painter or photographer and someone commissions you to take wedding photographs or paint a portrait? Does it still belong to you?

The easy answer is "don't go there". Have a contract and insert a condition to say who owns what. For instance, put a condition in the employment contract indicating that any IPR created by the employee during his employment belongs to the employer. For consultants a condition can be included in the contract assigning (i.e. legally allocating) the rights in any copyright work created by him during his retainer to the company paying his fee.

An important point to know is that copyright law can be overridden by agreement between the parties (there are exceptions to this but not many).

But what if you do not have a contract? There are some ground rules:

• Copyright works created by the employee within the course of business will belong to the employers. However a contractor/non-employee will own the copyright in any works he produces.

• A contract will save you a lot of trouble if anything of value is created and is worth fighting over. As a general rule the more complicated the problem you create the more it costs to sort it out.

• If the work is worth anything then the employee is likely to argue that the work was not created "within the normal course of business". In this case it is best to ask if the work was part of the normal duties of the employee. If not, even though he has used the employer's computers and other resources copyright may not belong to the employer. Employers may be astounded at this. However the courts have not been that sympathetic to the claims of employers trying to take literary works produced by their employees. However if you have set out the rights clearly in the employment or consultancy agreement the courts will enforce these rights. Courts do enforce agreements between parties even though they may not seem fair (see contract law later).

Sometimes it is difficult to tell a contractor from an employee. The court will decide on the basis of the control that the employer has over the way that the job is done, sharing of profit and any losses.

By the way, your wedding photographs are the copyright of the photographer unless of course you have a contract, which states otherwise.

8. The civil and criminal law (see later) protects copyright.

9. In general, copyright in a particular work – say a software programme – will last for the life of the author plus 70 years. In software this may seem an exceptionally long time however it is treated in a similar way to music and film. For instance, the length of time the protection lasts is very important to the Disney Corporation or the relatives of Elvis Presley.

10. Your work must be original.

If you have taken on board the above points then you have enough information on copyright to be dangerous. If you want more then read the following two advanced tips.

Tip A

In any conversation about copyright there is always a bit of a rush to get in the phrase "Copyright is the expression of the idea rather than the idea itself". If you can achieve this then you will probably frighten off people as it suggests you have a good grasp of the subject whereas most people *including* lawyers know very little.

Let me try to explain what this means. The protection applies to the way you put the words together not the idea itself. For example, if you are writing a novel then your idea might be girl meets boy, girl loses boy and then they get back together again. This basic plot is not copyright: that is the idea. You can't stop other people using the basic idea. However once you put it into writing then it has copyright as it is a literary work (provided it is original). Copyright protects the way you put the words together: *your* story.

Tip B

If someone else manages to say, "Copyright is the expression of the idea and not the idea" then all is not lost. A suitable reply is "it depends on the idea". This recognises that there has been case after case trying to separate the mere ideas from pretty full and complicated ideas which the courts have found to be copyright.

If the conversation goes any deeper that this, either feign illness or you can get away with nodding agreement. If asked any questions then clearly you must say that you will need to consider it. That is what I do even after years working in the area.

Copyright is like being in the freemasons: there are little signs to hint to other people that you know what you are talking about. Use the sign to someone who is not in the club and no damage is done. Use it to someone who knows something about copyright and you will have scored points. You may find this very good in job interviews.

2. Trade marks

A trademark is a sign used by a business like Coca-Cola® or IBM®. If you use the trademark in a way that jeopardises the guarantee of origin then that is a civil infringement. The guarantee of origin means that the purchaser knows that these goods came from this particular company. For instance, a coke bottle marked Coca-Cola® came from that company. If you misuse some other company's trademark in the course of a business then it is a criminal offence.

If you use another company's trademark on your web site which suggests that what you have to offer is somehow linked with that company when it is not then that is misuse. However, if you use another company's trademark on your web site to refer to their products then that is acceptable use.

Trademarks do not need to be registered in order to be protected. However in practice you should register your trademark or you will face great difficulty in protecting your trademark if another uses it. You must continue to use the trademark in business otherwise you may face a challenge from another user of the trademark "use it or lose it". An application period for a trademark takes 18 months or more.

You can tell if a trademark is registered, as you will usually see a ® beside the trademark this warns people off from using it. The application date is important as the registration protection starts from that date; sometimes you will see a ™ to denote that the "mark" is in the registration process. Once in that process the applicant can breathe a sigh of relief as far as other companies using the mark. However the process itself has hurdles.

The trademark registration will cover the UK so you can have the problem of other companies using your name overseas. There are registration processes covering the EU that is called a "community mark". You can also make an application that will cover most of the world under the "Madrid Protocol". It really is a matter of money and where you want to use it. However if a particular name is important to you it is a prudent idea to apply for registration before someone else does. The application that you make will not cover your name in every industry. You are asked to choose certain classes e.g. Class 16. The more classes you apply for, the more it costs, and the more chances that someone will object.

Trademarks are the easiest way to protect your products. All that you need to show in court is that someone has applied your trademark as opposed to proving that they infringed your copyright. For instance if someone is selling illegal software the software publisher will usually prosecute for infringement of a trade mark rather than face the difficult technical defences which are sometimes raised on infringement of copyright. In fact, once you have a trademark it is best to use it on the packaging and in the software itself so that a court action can be based on misuse of it. People who illegally copy your software may want to argue about a copyright claim that you have taken against them as there are many complex issues and loopholes. However if you have been smart with the placing of the trade marks in and on your products you have a lay down hand for a trade mark prosecution.

In conclusion, it is important to register trademarks.

3. Designs

In most cases designs such as icons and logos are protected automatically by copyright. However there is further IPR protection for designs called "design right". It can be registered or unregistered. There is a registered and unregistered design right system covering all of Europe. There is a very similar system just covering the UK. If you are just dealing in the UK it is cheaper to limit your registration to this country.

Unregistered design right provides protection for 3 years in Europe (15 years in the UK) and registered design right protection is up to 25 years.

Why not just rely on copyright? You should register your design for two reasons. First it is easier to prove. Secondly, it provides monopoly protection (similar to patents).

Everyone knows what a monopoly is. If you have a monopoly over a design then no one is able to reproduce that design without your permission for the stated period i.e. 25 years. If copyright is not a monopoly what is the protection offered? It is the right for your work not to be copied. If you do not register your design and rely on copyright protection then if someone independently comes up with the same design as you it is not a copyright infringement. They have not copied your design – they came up with the idea themselves. The fact that it is the same as your design is just a coincidence. They have not done anything wrong. So in the case of your 30 second doodle (which is probably a design too), you are both entitled to sell, give licences for and generally exploit the doodle. If only you had registered your doodle as a design, then no one would be permitted to use it for 25 years. *Note:* unregistered design right does not grant monopoly protection.

I warned you that copyright was a pain the neck. In copyright nothing is really straightforward. This is another reason to register your design. From this you can guess one of the popular defences to copyright claims: the defendant claims that he was unaware of your work and the doodle was his own idea.

If you can understand the copying versus monopoly concept you are doing really well.

Last word on designs. If you have a hot design, don't start exhibiting or marketing it without getting some legal advice. If you put your design in the public domain you could lose the right to register it. Having said that designers do get one year's grace from the time of disclosure to register the design. However delay in registration can end in tears.

4. Patents

Patents are granted for inventions. If you can imagine the type of invention produced by a nutty professor then that is in general what patents cover. For instance, the light bulb, telephone or a Dyson® vacuum cleaner. It must be original. Patents provide a 20-year protection.

There are four things to know about patents:

1. A patent, unlike copyright, is a form of monopoly. If you invent a special type of potato peeler then no one else can manufacturer that peeler for 20 years. This gives time to exploit your invention. In the same way as a registered design.

2. Patents are registered. An important point to know about patents is that if you start using the invention or publicising it before you have applied for a patent then you may not get any protection at all. If you have made an invention get a lawyer or patent agent involved to help make sure it does not lose the protection.

3. Generally speaking in Europe, patent protection is not
    available for software unless it contains some technical
    innovation, which would equate to an invention. However, in
    practice there are a lot of software patents which somehow
    pass through this process. The law is likely to be changed in
    favour of software patents. In the USA anything that moves
    can be patented or so it seems compared to the European
    system. One patent covers one country. If you want your
    product to be protected by patent in any other countries then
    you must register your patent in each of those countries.

4. Patents are subject to strict formality and are expensive not
    only to register but also to enforce in the courts. One senior
    lawyer tells his clients that they need £500,000 to see a patent
    action through. If they lose then they also have the
    defendants' costs. This expense works both ways. If you start
    selling a product that is protected by another person's patent
    and they take legal action then you will lose a great deal of
    money just in legal costs. Patent cases tend to settle as the
    parties run out of will to fund the legal action.

5. Databases

There is a database right protecting the content of a database for
15 years. Regularly updating a database may extend this limitation
period indefinitely.

Summary

Now you know more about IPR than over 99% of the UK
population. I hope that feels good.

In summary, IPR can earn your company a lot of money and should
be treated seriously. They have strong legal protection – so bear that
in mind if you should interfere with the IPR of another company.

CHAPTER 2
THE REST OF THE LAW – IN BRIEF

There are eight other laws about which the IT Professional should have an understanding. They are:

1. Pornography

Pornography in general

Pornographers have been fundamental to the development of the internet. With the support and finance of organised crime the pornographer was one of the first to grasp the opportunities of e-business. They pioneered internet methods of marketing, direct mailing and secure payment. This illegal use has sparked the interest of the police in the internet and there are now an increasing number of specialised Child Protection/Hi Tech Crime Units operating worldwide like the one at Scotland Yard. Of the 75,000 paedophiles identified by a recent US internet operation on a US site over 7,000 were from the UK. It is the police interest in paedophiles and the apparent high incidence of this crime which increases the risk for business that their resources are being used in an illegal manner.

The main thing to note is that pornography is not illegal: it is only certain types of pornograpy which involve obscenity and/or paedophilia that are crimes meriting imprisonment. However companies face a major issue here and IT Professionals must have policies and the know-how to alert their management and deal with the problem.

There are a number of Acts that IT Professionals should be aware of the most important of which is the Obscene Publications Act

1959. This would involve the distribution of pornography say within a company. However it has to "deprave and corrupt". This is given the usual dictionary meaning. This is not much help but as one judge commented: "I cannot describe it but I know what it is when I see it". It has got to be something pretty bad to merit a prosecution under this Act in this day and age. I don't know of any criminal prosecutions of company employees downloading this sort of thing.

A further bar to prosecution is that it needs to be done *for gain*: simple possession is not enough. Policies should make it clear that downloading pornography (illegal or legal) is not allowed. Failure to include this ban in your policies may make it difficult to justify any dismissal resulting from the use at work of pornography which is not illegal (see *Employment Tribunals* at page 50 below).

There is always the possibility of another employee taking action for being exposed to pornography in the workplace. It has been long established that employees especially female staff should not be subjected to phonographic images in the work place. Such an employee could claim that exposure to such an image amounted to constructive dismissal. It would allow the employee to make a claim as if she has been unfairly dismissed.

The danger for business is that the police can obtain a warrant for search and seizure of obscene articles and any supporting evidence such as the computers if they suspect such items to be on your premises or more likely within your computers.

It is the prosecution in an obscene publication case which must prove beyond reasonable doubt that the defendant knew what he was doing.

All in all a police intervention for pornography by itself is unlikely.

Pornography Involving Children

However it is a very different matter in cases relating to images of children.

There are two Acts dealing with paedophilia: the Protection of Children Act 1978 and the Criminal Justice Act 1988. These Acts deal with distributing, downloading and possessing of indecent images of children. If an employee is downloading indecent pictures of children, then this could spell trouble not only for the employee but also for the IT Manager. The definition of children being under the age of 16.

Once the prosecution can prove that the indecent images of children were on a computer of which you had control then it is up to you to prove your innocence. This is a reverse of the usual standard of being innocent until proven guilty.

An IT Professional is usually the person who discovers the indecent images or is tasked to investigate. He must be very careful in dealing with the indecent images to ensure that he does not commit an offence. When being faced with such a serious offence the employee may try to blame someone else such as the IT Manager.

The statutory defences are that the suspect (that could be you):

- had a legitimate reason (e.g. being a policeman), or

- had not seen the photograph or had no reason to suspect they were indecent; or

- that the photograph was sent to you without any prior request and that it was not kept by you for an unreasonable period of time.

This places the IT Professional in a "Catch 22" situation. If he stores indecent images to keep as evidence then he could be charged with an offence. However if he does not keep the evidence then the company may lose a claim for unfair dismissal in the absence of the evidence. The answer is: do not to keep the images unless it is to hand them over to police straight away. They must be treated like a hot potato. But what if your company does not want to involve the police but wishes to dismiss the employee and are concerned that without the offending images you may lose in an employment tribunal? There is too much risk in keeping the images. It is better to try and explain to an employment tribunal why you destroyed the images because if you lose you only risk a financial award being made against your company. The alternative is for the IT Manager to try and explain to a criminal court why he had indecent images. In the latter case the IT Manager risks imprisonment and his name being entered onto the Sexual Offenders Register.

Look out for offensive material on your systems: it can lead to trouble.

2. Strict liability

Generally in law you are not responsible for something unless you have done something wrong. In criminal law that generally means that you intended the act to be done. In civil law you can be liable if the injury or damage was caused through your negligence rather than your intentional act; for example if you failed to fix a paving stone on your property and someone tripped over and was injured.

However sometimes the law goes further than this and imposes strict liability.

Strict liability is where you are liable even if you did not intend the act to happen nor were you negligent. For instance if you have a illicit copy of a software application on your computer even if you did not know it was there, you have committed a copyright infringement. Now if you are a company with 1,000s of software applications on your computer network it may seem unfair to make you responsible. However, it may be unreasonable to make the software publisher who owns the application prove that you knew it was there.

Other examples of strict liability are where an employee is injured at work the employer is normally liable without the employee proving that the employer knew of the danger or was negligent. Or when a company sells a defective product and someone is injured.

Strict liability may not seem fair. Just as ignorance of the law is no excuse. "I did not know" is also not always a sufficient defence.

3. Vicarious liability

I am often asked by IT Professionals to explain the concept of vicarious liability.

Vicarious liability is a type of strict liability. It is part of the civil law. An employer can be sued where his employee has done something wrong in the course of business.

There are good practical reasons for making the employer responsible for its employees. They are:

- The employer has money and probably insurance cover.

- It is easier to identify the employer e.g. if a Dell store man drops a computer on your foot then who would you want to sue? Even if you did have the satisfaction of winning a civil action against a store man he is likely to have little money to compensate you. In law penniless people – those who it is not worth suing – are called "Men of Straw".

- Employers need to be reminded to make their systems safe and are in a better position to do so than the employee.

- The employee is still liable if he has been negligent but usually the victim goes straight to the employers. It is unusual for the employer to sue the employee for the trouble that they may have caused. However this option is open to employers.

So vicarious liability is a common sense rule, there is nothing mystical or theoretical about it.

The company is usually responsible for negligence by its contractors or other people or agents carrying out the company's business. Companies may succeed by arguing that they are not responsible for casual workers but this is an uphill struggle. A rule of thumb is that if the negligent party truly has his own separate business then he will be solely liable. However there are many people called "consultants" who are in truth employees as they only work for one company and in every other way look like employees of the company. Courts increasingly come down on the victim's side and will find someone to pay. For instance, there is a duty to instruct competent independent contractors. There have been a lot of court cases over the years so if you are involved in either side of this situation expect an argument.

A big part of the argument is whether or not the employee was engaged in the company's business. For example, if a lorry driver takes a detour to have a cup of tea with his girlfriend and knocks someone over on the way, he has gone off on a frolic of his own. This is not company business so technically the employer should not be responsible. The test that a court would apply in order to decide if the employee was acting in the course of employment is: were the employee's acts so closely connected to his employment that it makes no difference? So here a detour of a few miles may still make the employer liable for the accident however if the driver took his girlfriend to the seaside for the day then it is unlikely that the employer will be liable. Having said that, I repeat that the court will look for someone to pay the injured person for the damage caused. The employer will still be liable even if the employee's action was unauthorised or unjustified e.g. there was a case where a lorry driver delivering petrol to a petrol station lit a cigarette causing an explosion and the employer was still liable. The safest course is to assume that however stupid your employees are the employer is responsible for what they do. This is very comforting for the dumber employee and the reason why most prudent employers have insurance. This is so even if the employer has expressly forbidden the employee from doing the terrible thing that has happened.

However, that is not to say that you should admit liability for your employee's acts as cases can go either way.

A bus conductor who punched a rude customer was found not to be acting in the course of his employment. Nor was a cleaning service company for an employee cleaner who made long distance calls at a customer's premises. Nor was the Fire Authority responsible for firemen who went on a go-slow on the way to a burning building, as this was tantamount to refusing to do the job. However a bouncer that attacked a customer with a cosh was thought to be acting in the course of business although in an excessive way.

An employer was not liable for an employee who gave a lift to a non-employee when the non-employee was injured. However a milkman who had a 13 year old helping him on his round made the milk company vicariously liable to the boy when he was injured as a result of the milkman's negligent driving.

4. Defamation – a Third Rail Issue

The expression "3rd rail issue" came from the New York subway where the subway trains ran on three rails. There are two ordinary rails and then a third one that is electrified. Step on the 3rd rail and you are electrocuted.

Defamation is a "3rd rail issue". It will get you fired and make all involved haemorrhage money.

Did you know that England is one of the best jurisdictions in which to bring defamation proceedings? Most people would think it would be the USA. In 1996 a well-known Russian businessman, Mr. Boris Berezovsky, was the subject of a highly critical article by *Forbes*, an American magazine. It suggested that he was the "Godfather of the Kremlin". Now instead of suing in America, Mr. Berezovsky chose England. He explained: "In this country, if you say I am an elephant you have to prove it. In America I have to prove that I am not an elephant". What is the situation in the UK if you or one of your employees makes a defamatory comment about a rival? It is only necessary for the rival to produce the email (to prove it was said and was published) then it is up to you to prove either it is true or it is a fair comment to make. In America the onus to prove that the comment is derogatory is on the rival.

Defamation is exactly what you think it is. Saying something nasty about someone else. In fact there are two ways to defame someone: by the spoken word (which is slander) and the written word (which is called libel). The main thing to know about defamation is not to do it. However a company is responsible for its employees not doing it too. There lies the problem: how to stop employees from defaming others or for the company to distance itself from those comments. A tip is that if you are going to defame someone it is better to be slander than libel as it is far more difficult for the claimant to prove what was said. Put those comments in an email and it can be a "lay down hand" for the claimant. The Norwich Union insurance company in 1997 had an employee who committed to email derogatory comments about the financial viability of Western Provident. Norwich Union were sued and had to pay a £450,000 settlement. It may have been the status of the company and the financial implications of any adverse comment about its financial stability which may have made this settlement sum so high. Damages are a payment to put the injured party back in the place they would have been in if the email had not been published. Damages are not to punish: that is left to the criminal law. Therefore the Norwich Union case is exceptional as the content of the email must have been very serious. No doubt the reader has heard of this case but should know that although civil proceedings were commenced it did not get to a trial it was settled at one of the preliminary hearings. The great thing about defamation is that there is such a low barrier to entry. You do not need any elaborate tools you just need to open your big mouth. Looking around your own company, no doubt, you can find a lot of employees capable of that.

Calling another person's company's CEO "big nose" is not in the same class as the Norwich Union case. Hurt pride is not worth very much in damages! Often defamation actions are fought out for a very low reward. Damages can be as low as 1p. However that 1p award means that the claimant has won. The winning party normally gets an order for costs against the losing party. So, the losing party will need to pay his own costs and the winner's costs. This is enough to bankrupt most individuals. The shareholders of your company are unlikely to want to take this sort of risk.

However to succeed in law, the defamation must be published. Basically it needs to be sent to at least one other. The wider it is published, e.g. on the internet, where the publication could be to the whole on-line world, then the more the damages there may be. So the IT Manager – like it or not – is the gatekeeper. He can stop it by implementing policies and making sure other employees are aware of them. Most of us learn to keep our mouths shut.

But the boot is not always on the foot of the injured party. The cost of defamation proceedings puts most people out of the game.

It runs at £500,000 for each party. It is difficult to be exact, as litigation is an open chequebook.

Whereas the costs should rule most people out of the game, in my experience even in my general law practice, I found many people would go to a solicitor to fire a few opening shots over the bows (usually of their neighbours). Even though they have not got the money to commence an action. This is started by a letter setting out the facts requesting an immediate apology in a form of a draft letter attached. Some request a published apology.

Even though no one in his or her right mind would commence a defamation action, it is best to cut this type of thing off at the pass. Assuming that the statement is defamatory it is usually best to make an apology and move on. The classic legal stance of admit nothing can make things worse as a court in awarding costs and damages will take into account an apology sincerely made.

If your company's business has been damaged significantly in commercial terms and your reputation is on the line and you may lose a very substantial sum of money: then defamation proceedings are a consideration. However if it is a matter of deep insult then it is usually not worth going beyond the initial solicitor's letter and if the culprit is crazy enough to call your bluff he may be crazy enough to waste a lot of his and your money on lawyers' fees. George Carmen, the eminent defamation barrister, said of defamation proceedings "the risks far outweigh the rewards" and he was a man who made his money from it. Also, in defamation proceedings Mr Carmen said that "the private life of all concerned were fair game and your own cupboard had best be free of skeletons".

It is crucial to drive home to your employees the importance of not making defamatory statements.

What to tell your employees

Make sure they know: *making defamatory statements will get them fired.*

Put this in policies and include it in staff training.

Suing and Being Sued – Some Considerations

There are three steps to take if there is a complaint against your company about a defamatory statement:

1. If you receive a solicitor's letter do nothing until you have spoken to your lawyers.

2. Apologise early and move on.

3. Say nothing further to inflame the situation as you cannot afford to defend proceedings.

There are three things to bear in mind if you are defamed:

1. You cannot afford to take proceedings.

2. Sending a solicitor's letter demanding an apology is probably as far as you go.

3. If your bluff is called, forget it except in exceptional circumstances.

Of course, if you have money to spare and want to spend it on court proceedings then that is a different matter.

5. Contract Law – Ten Things to Know

Contract is a voluminous area of law which applies to the daily dealings of the IT Professional. Common sense and logic only go so far in interpreting the law and in some cases things are a certain way because the law says so.

Here are ten things that IT Professionals should know about contract law:

1. If you sign something then saying you didn't read it is no defence.

2. A "deal is a deal". If you entered into a contract then the courts are probably going to force you to go through with it however

bad the deal turns out to be. You will have an uphill task in trying to get out of a contract. Therefore exercise caution before agreeing to anything. More importantly have systems to stop employees committing you to expensive and unnecessary purchases.

3.   A contract does not need to be in writing. For example, if one person says "Do you want this item for £1?" and the other person says "yes", that is a contract. However, it is hard to prove.

4.   The same applied where you "click" to accept (a "click wrap" agreement).

5.   Always get contracts in writing to stop people denying they ever made any agreement.

6.   Don't promise things which are not true. If you do induce a person to enter into a contract by making an untrue statement then that other party may be able to get out of the contract. This is called a misrepresentation.

7.   A contract by email or fax is just as good as hard copy. For example, someone sends you an email "Do you want x for £1?" you answer by email "yes". Then that is a contract and you are committed.

8.   You must be alerted to the terms of the contract before you agree. If they tell you about the terms after you agree they do not apply. This can be done by telling you there are terms and conditions that apply. They do not need to show the terms and conditions to you but they can simply tell you where they can be obtained (e.g. bus ticket normally refers to conditions, but we don't read them on the step of the bus).

9.   If services are provided to you before the contract is signed/agreed. Then there is no contract and technically you do not need to pay. However courts will often order you to make payment for services provided to you where you received benefit.

10. If someone sends you a product without you having ordered it. You can keep it under the Unsolicited Goods Act.

In all the above statements there are ifs and buts. The law is full of exceptions. Sorry. However these 10 statements will be a good starting point in any argument.

6. Human Rights is Hype

There has been a lot said lately about human rights. However in practice the Human Rights legislation does not really affect the average UK business. The Human Rights Convention was signed after the second world war to protect citizens from governments/ states overstepping their powers.

So an arrested drunk railing against the police saying "I know my rights, this is against my human rights" is a correct use of Human Rights. This is because the police and other government bodies are public authorities and the Human Rights Convention is intended to keep such government type bodies in line. A court is also a public authority and it will need to bear in mind the Human Rights legislation.

However an employee railing against the IT Manager, of a commercial business, that he has abused his human rights is not correct usage. The IT Manager is not a public authority. Such employees should be complaining about a breach of UK legislation which was brought in as a result of the Human Rights principles such as the role of RIPA in the monitoring of email (see RIPA later).

Some other facts about the human rights legislation are:

*   This Human Rights Convention provided for the European Court of Justice, this is nothing to do with the European Union. It is to this court that appeals can be made concerning treatment of UK citizens. Human rights cases often seem to involve sex and violence of one type or another. Other complaints refer to UK legislation which is not in keeping with the principles of the human rights convention.

*   The Human Rights Act 1998 was passed in the UK and this will stop a lot of cases going to Europe to be heard.

So the next time an employee starts shouting about breaches of Human Rights you can confidently say: "So what". However you should be worried when employees start shouting about data protection, RIPA or other legislation spawned by the principles of the Human Rights Convention.

7. Distance Selling – All You Need to Know

The key rules are in the Distance Selling Consumer Protection (Distance Selling) Regulations 2000. These set out some basic rules that European Union countries have agreed to for dealing with consumers when trading on the internet or shopping by phone or mail order.

The company selling is expected to send the goods within 30 days of the order.

The consumer gets a cooling off period of seven days to withdraw from the contract. This will start after he receives the goods. However if the seller of the goods hasn't confirmed what the buyer is getting in writing then the cooling off period will be delayed until that is done.

There are a number of common sense exceptions to this cancellation right including software or like goods that have been opened.

The regulations do not apply to auctions.

8. Dealing in Other Jurisdictions and Cross Border Sales

You make a deal in the UK with a Frenchman living in Germany to sell a product which is to be delivered to and used in Canada. The invoice is to be submitted to the US parent. The Frenchman says that the product did not work and payment is refused. He is lying. What do you do?

Whereas this was a scenario confined to law examinations a few years ago, with the advent of the internet this is commonplace.

Fortunately the answer is still the same. If you want to try your hand at litigation this is probably not the case as the complexity adds up to a lot of expense for you. Certainly threaten court action (although even this can backfire in some cases). Hire a lawyer to write letters. But hesitate before issuing proceedings and do not expect miracles.

Having said that there will be times when the IT Professional has to grapple with this issue (see Chapter 9: The Internet at page 94).

CHAPTER 3
THE LAW AND THE COURTS

It is easy to confuse criminal law and civil law. However, the penalties that each type of law imposes are very different.

For the IT Professional the importance of the difference between the two is that, Professionals should get the terminology right if they are to sound credible. I often hear people mixing up the various terms. Fortunately, it is not difficult to learn the difference between the two laws. Probably the more important distinction between the criminal and civil law is how worried you should be if someone threatens your company or you with action under either law. A basic understanding of the difference will allow you to assess the credibility of the threat which is being made against you.

There follows a basic explanation of the differences between the criminal and the civil law and how these laws are applied to the protection of IPR.

1. Civil law

This is where one person sues another in a "civil action". Rather than a criminal "prosecution".

There are basically two different types of civil court. These are: the County Court which deal with the bulk of civil cases and the High Court which deals with the more serious cases.

A claimant must prove his case "on the balance of probabilities". This means that the judge will make up his mind on the basis of the facts he has heard as to what he believes has happened. No jury is involved in most civil cases.

Something important for you to note is that the word "fine" is not used in civil law. An order by the court for a defendant to pay a sum of money is called "damages". For instance, a court could order the defendant to pay an award of damages in the sum of £10,000. An award of damages is money paid directly to the successful claimant whereas a fine is money which is paid to the court and into state funds.

The other types of orders that can be made by a civil court are costs, injuctions and civil search orders.

An example of a civil case would be if you sold your old computer to someone for £30.00 and they would not give you the money. Then you could sue in a civil court and be awarded damages of £30.00.

In civil courts sometimes the blame for the injury is not clear. For instance, in a car accident where both parties are to blame. In these cases the court can order that the claimant is "contributory negligent" and reduce the payment made to the defendant by a percentage of the total damages.

An important point to note is that the civil law is not used to punish the defendant. It is used to put the claimant back in the position that he would have been in if the accident or damage had not occurred. For instance, if a person would not pay for your computer then the correct amount to award is £30.00. Even if the person owing the money has behaved very badly. There would still be no extra payment ordered to reflect this as this would be punishment.

Civil proceedings are usually very expensive to mount and defend. The "costs" are the legal expenses of the parties to the action. The general rule is that the losing parties pays the winning parties legal costs. This can be a considerable penalty on the losing party. It should be noted that even when the winning sides costs are paid by the losing side this usually does not cover more than a proportion, say, 75% of the total bill of the winning side. The winner must still find 25% of the costs to pay to his solicitors. So starting a legal action should not be seen as a licence to make money. What happens if the losing side does not have any or enough money? A court order for damages is made and stands. However if the defendant does not have the money then you must pay your own lawyers until such time you can get the money from the defendant or decide to give up.

If one party to a civil action is not happy with the result he can appeal to a higher court. These courts are called the Court of Appeal and the House of Lords.

2. Criminal law

The criminal law is used by the state to punish people. The defendant is called upon to plead guilty or not guilty. There is a trial which can be before a deputy judge or magistrate in the Magistrates' Courts or in usually more serious matters before a judge with a jury in the Crown Court.

Once the trial is finished the jury will announce its verdict whether or not the defendant is guilty or not guilty. In the Magistrates' Court the judge or magistrate decides if the defendant is guilty or not guilty.

The "prosecution" must prove their case "beyond reasonable doubt". This means that the judge or jury must be *sure* that the defendant is guilty. It is not just to decide what most probably happened. This is a higher burden than in the civil courts.

Where it has been decided that the defendant is guilty, the judge then decides the sentence. The court can fine the defendant or impose a term of imprisonment or one of the alternatives to imprisonment e.g. community service, probation etc.. These are criminal penalties and can only be imposed by the criminal courts.

Any convictions imposed by a criminal court means that the person has a criminal record. If you lose in a civil court the judgement is recorded but it is not added to your criminal record.

3. The civil law applied to IPR

Now that you have been patient enough to trawl through the differences between the criminal and civil law we come to the importance of the differences for you as an IT professional, taking different types of action in turn.

Copyright infringement

Damages. As you now know this is a financial payment ordered by the court. It is not a fine and not intended to punish. It is awarded to put the claimant back in the position that he would have been in if the software had not been copied. So what would be the civil damages if you are caught using one copy of a software program? The damages (money) awarded can be quite low; perhaps payment for a new copy (assuming that it is to continue in use) and payment for past use of the software. This will depend on the price and the extent of the use. Most cases of software infringement settle before they go to court. If the infringer can prove that he did not know that the software was someone else's copyright and that he had no reason to know then the court would not award damages at all. The infringer would simply be ordered to stop using it and give it back to the rightful owner. This would be difficult to prove where you were caught with an unpaid for commercial software package.

Now you know the rule that civil law damages do not punish I must confess there are some exceptions. In breach of copyright the court can award additional damages if the use was flagrant.

Civil Search order. This is where the software publisher can get an order in the civil court to search your office. The court can grant the order without your knowledge. The courts do not make such orders lightly. However where it is suspected that you will destroy the evidence or the records of your misuse then the courts may grant such an order. As the evidence will be from your own employee, that employee may not give such a favourable account of your respect for law and order. But the claimant must be careful if he puts before the court facts that are not true even if he is relying on what has been told to him as he may be ordered to pay costs.

Doorstep order – this again is granted in the absence of the defendant and is intended to take him by surprise. The software publisher can attend at your office and request certain records and evidence to be handed over then and there. This order is often obtained instead of a search order.

Injunction This is an order for you to stop using the copyright work e.g. software. This can be disastrous for a business. Injunctions are a common order for copyright infringement. They are often granted without the defendant's knowledge. The court will consider if damages ordered at trial rather than stopping the defendants use would be sufficient. The court will look at the use from the position of the claimant and the defendant. For instance when a software publisher's software was deliberately incorporated into software owned by another company and being sold. If this is damaging the product then the court will order an injunction to stop it. However if the claimant's business is not affected by the use then the court can allow the matter to go to trial on the basis that if the claimant is successful he can take the profits from the defendant.

The injunction order is made with a court return date (within a few days of service of the order). The court will then decide if the injunction is to continue having heard what the defendant has to say.

Costs As you know in civil proceedings these can be the real penalty. Copyright is a very expensive area of the law to stumble into. The law firms acting for software publishers tend to be expert and expensive. Injunction is a very common tool – you can imagine that a law firm preparing a case which must be brought to court in a matter of 1–2 days will charge extra for the emergency nature of the hearing. It usually takes place in the more expensive High Court. There is not only the initial hearing but also the return hearing. In one recent case a small publisher estimated his costs as £30,000 in two months.

There are situations where you will know nothing about the possibility of a civil action until you receive an injunction order. However in most cases the intention of the claimant to take you to court will be loud and clear.

Civil actions are expensive. It is best to instruct a solicitor who knows how the system works and can speak on your behalf without letting emotion get the way.

To ignore letters or to tell the claimant to get lost may well end you in court.

4. The criminal law applied to IRP

The software publisher in pursuing a copyright infringement can choose either a civil or criminal action.

When faced with a criminal prosecution the risk is a criminal record.

For prosecuting individuals selling software commercially by either counterfeiting or unlawful copying then software publishers' enforcement bodies (such as FAST) will work with Trading Standards officers.

For straightforward under licensing (otherwise usually respectable businesses buying once and copying it many times) criminal prosecutions are rare. But this ability to choose a criminal route sets an infringement of copyright apart from the usual business disputes over failure to meet the terms of a contract, such as debt collection, where only a civil remedy is available. For instance, I know of a software publisher which produced an address system. It was very successful. One company bought a number of licences but found that their employees were so impressed with the product that they copied the system throughout their business. The software publisher became aware of this misuse and although being flattered at the use was losing thousands of pounds. They asked the company to count the copies in use and pay up. The purchasing company wanted to renegotiate the price as they were using considerably more copies that they had originally ordered they argued that they should get a cheaper deal. They were of a size where they normally dictated the terms of a deal so were quite prepared to let the software publisher sweat. However, by using more copies than they had paid for they were committing a copyright infringement. By continuing to use the software after they became aware that they were using more that they had paid for is a civil infringement but also a criminal offence. In these circumstances the software publisher got paid the full price and did not pursue a criminal prosecution. However the point is that the purchasing department had taken the risk of the prosecution and were relying on the software publisher's business sense and goodwill not to take a private prosecution. A more prudent company would not have placed themselves in that position. Not all software publishers are beacons of business sense and goodwill. So be warned.

Therefore a company which regularly receives demonstration copies from software publishers (such as IT magazines, which are supplied) to enable the publication to evaluate the software products. Has the problem of the licence usually stating that the product can only be used in a certain way.

A company which receives a font usually attached to an email or downloaded by the marketing department is receiving software. A font in itself is too short to be protected unless it is a design or has significant artist quality. However most fonts today are driven by software such as Adobe® Postscript. Companies such as AGFA Monotype are copyright holders of fonts and they want to discourage this free for all use. It is estimated that 40% of font software in use is without the appropriate licence. They have both civil and criminal remedies at their disposal.

A copyright infringement can be a criminal offence where it is done in the course of business. This allows infringements committed by individuals at home or as a hobby to be excluded from the criminal law (but caught by the civil law). There are exceptions when the dealing is so extensive that it amounts to a commercial enterprise. Some school children have been known to expand their hobby from their bedroom to an extent which adds up to a commercial concern.

If you have unlicenced software in your business (as many businesses do) this puts the IT Manager in a difficult position. The criminal law normally requires a person not only to know of the crime but to participate in it. However criminal copyright only requires the Director or person in the managerial position to turn a blind eye to "connive" at the use. In addition an employee can be criminally liable for possessing a copy.

Increasingly IT Managers and employees in otherwise legitimate businesses look to the employer to have paid for the software being used. Why should they take the chance of a criminal conviction?

The enforcement bodies settle most matters. However it is their goodwill that is stopping people being taken to court. The enforcement bodies were behind recent initiatives which increased the penalties from 2 to 10 years' imprisonment. They will always be on the look out for cases that can be used as an example to others.

There are similar criminal provisions in other countries. These provide for an offence if an infringing copy is made for sale or hire, imported (for business) provided the person knows or has reason to believe the copy is infringing. Also if he possesses in the course of business with a view to committing any infringing act.

Most prosecutions for software are pursued under the trademark legislation, as it is easier. However there is a defence if the defendant did not know or have reason to believe that the trademark was an infringement. Conviction can lead to imprisonment for 10 years and an unlimited fine. In practice sentences of 18 months are not unusual for organised operators.

**PART 2
THE ENEMY WITHIN
– EMPLOYEES AND CONSULTANTS**

CHAPTER 4
KEEPING AN EYE ON YOUR STAFF

1. Monitoring Employees Communications
– RIPA the basics

The Regulation of Investigatory Powers Act 2000 ("RIPA") (with regulations) puts the interception of communications on a statutory footing and ensures compliance with the Human Rights legislation.

It came about as a result of a 1997 case where a Ms. Halford who was a senior police officer in Liverpool was in dispute with her employer. Her private calls made from inside police premises on the police private network were monitored. Until then it was accepted that interception of public telephone calls was unlawful but this did not apply to a private network. She applied to the European Court of Justice which ruled that under the Convention of Human Rights she had a right of respect for her privacy from interception of her calls by a public authority such as the police.

RIPA makes it a criminal offence to intercept calls from a private telephone system such as your office telephone system unless the person has a right to control the system or has the consent of the person making the call.

IT Professionals can face civil liability for unauthorised interception by the person who has a right to control the system or person whose privacy has been violated.

A company monitoring its employees' calls *with their consent* is acceptable. However companies should not go over the top in monitoring the calls or emails of their employees.

What is probably *not* over the top:

–   Monitoring incoming calls for training or record purposes provided that is reasonable and the callers are told;

–   Occasionally looking at employees' emails or listening to calls to make sure they are not abusing the system.

Acceptability depends on the industry the company is in and the objective of the monitoring. Banks will require a high level of monitoring whereas a Big Brother type regime in a trading company's office (as much as it may please the architect of the system) is over the top!

But companies should include a clear statement of their intention in their policies and make sure employees know this is the practice. Just be aware that you open your company up to potential claims if you go too far.

The act allows law enforcement agencies to get permission to monitor. It also provides for a statutory framework for surveillance by police etc.

Warrant

Most IT Professionals worry that one day a policemen will demand data from them. The easy answer to that is that they must have an interception warrant: so ask to see it. The only situation where they can demand data from you without a warrant is where they have the consent of one of the parties to the communication being intercepted and the surveillance was authorised under the Act. Where there is no warrant you should be sceptical and you may feel more comfortable with assurance from a more senior police officer.

2.   Email Monitoring is Essential

Sex, harassment and gossip are rife in corporate life. Yet corporations adhere to the convenient fiction that their employees are whiter than white. Such a policy is no longer viable.

It is time for corporations to look beyond their own sometimes ridicuously pious corporate value statements and take a reality check.

For many years, corporations have pretended that bad habits don't exist in their workforce and that policy has worked. No investigations meant few problems came to light. The occasional scapegoat employee was sacrificed.

What has changed is:

1) Employees' commitment and ability to record, circulate and store evidence of these bad habits and inappropriate statements in *email and the corporate network*.

2) Access on the internet to *illegal or inappropriate material* (pornography and illegal software)

3) The *ability to retrieve this information* is not only enhanced by system/forensic techniques but also the simple £10 data access request (see Data Subject Access Request below).

4) Victims are not prepared to keep quiet, supported by a news-hungry and fearless *press*.

5) The *compensation culture* is flamed by corporations' reluctance to be involved in litigation.

The fallout for companies is:

- *Increased employment tribunals proceedings*. The damages that employees can expect have been raised to £50K which makes employees far more likely to take issue if they should be subject to harassment or bullying.

- *Data subject access requests* under the Data Protection Act are a very cheap, informal and seemingly extensive form of disclosure of documents concerning what has been said about that employee.

- *Police investigations* – warrants are rapidly granted to police to enter corporate premises at any suggestion of child pornography.

IT Professionals who hang on to such material can be themselves liable under the act (see *Pornography* above).

- *Defamation proceedings*. It cost Norwich Union £450K plus their own costs to settle a defamation action which started due to an email rumour that their employees started about another companies financial viability.

- *Bad publicity*. A sexually explicit email forwarded by one solicitor to another was soon copied millions of times.

- *The "smoking gun" email*. This is all aided by the increasingly commonplace smoking gun email in legal cases. It is common in litigation for disclosure to take place. This is the procedure where both sides produce all documents (including letters, emails) to the other party. It is now a regular occurrence to find an email blowing your case out of the water. Employees like to place criticism of projects in emails.

Companies can either wait for this potential tidal wave to occur or take preventative action. Many of the problems stem from employees trying to be funny. I am not suggesting that humour be banned in the workplace although that may seem, at times, the HR Department's preferred option.

Part of the solution is the increased monitoring of staff email, but the legislation leaves IT Professionals crying out for simple guidelines.

FAST, which runs a program in the UK and the US for companies to become voluntarily software compliant, has issued guidelines to help its members to keep email under control.

FAST's 10 Email Monitoring Guidelines

1. No pornography allowed.

2. Frankly inform employees of the monitoring policy.

3. Advise employees to protect their privacy by deleting personal emails (if such emails are permitted).

4. Restrict and/or regulate employees storage of email.

5. Do not open personal email.

6. Act on personal data revealed if it shows gross misconduct or crime otherwise ignore it.

7. If necessary, monitor absent employees but do not record.

8. Document awareness programs.

9. Give employees the opportunity to explain their conduct.

10. Do not go over the top – balance business risk against employee privacy.

The FAST 10 Email Monitoring Guidelines for IT Managers:

1. *Rule one....No porno*

The dangers of pornography are dealt with elsewhere in this book. However the risk is well illustrated in the case of email misuse.

High minded corporate value statements encouraging zero tolerance policies have caused well publicised mass sackings of employees for using pornography. However morally satisfying a purge may be, what can be a good way of getting rid of troublesome employees sets a precedent that must be applied to the good employees too. It is better to accept that some employees would like to do this if they could get away with it. It is a matter of convincing them the monitoring system is such that they will be caught. Dismissal in the run of the mill case is not necessary.

2. *Frankly inform employees of the monitoring policy*

"This call is monitored for training purposes". In other words "we spy on our employees to ensure they treat customers well and do not misbehave". If employees are going to stop putting the company at risk they are going to need to get used to a more frank approach. Monitoring should not be done on the sly or as undercover surveillance.

Involve employees and unions in drawing up the policy. The same is true of all monitoring of employees communications.

3. *If personal email is permitted advise employees to protect their privacy by deleting personal emails*

You make employees responsible for their own belongings at work the same rule should be applied to their email. They can send it home and delete it.

4. *Restrict and/or regulate employees storage of email*

A court action against one of the largest software publishers suggested the dangers of smoking gun emails. The best way to avoid this is to tightly control storage whilst having a culture that deters employees from making inappropriate remarks in emails. Some industries are regulated so that they must keep all communications for a number of years. In these companies an efficient email storage system is essential.

5. *Do not open personal email*

There may well be exceptions to this but as a general rule obviously personal emails are potentially a can of worms.

6. Act on personal data revealed if it shows gross misconduct or crime, otherwise ignore it

The IT Professional should be cautious but not timid. You want the IT Professional to be seen to be bold if he is going to prevent employees risking misbehaviour. A good monitoring policy will support firm action. However if the IT Professional becomes aware of information of a clearly personal nature, then he does not need to dwell on it.

7. If necessary, monitor absent employees' inboxes

Business does not stop when the employee goes on vacation.

8. Document awareness programs

When problems arise, employees usually deny knowing the policy existed. Awareness programs can include employee contacts, intranets, boot camps, training days, tasks that require signing or acknowledging changes.

9. Give employees the opportunity to explain the conduct

Sometimes the most suspicious circumstances can have a reasonable explanation.

10. Do not go over the top-balance business risk against employee privacy

Whilst wishing to be seen to be firm an officious IT Professional can be part of the problem rather than part of the solution.

Will this make the employees initially feel uncomfortable? Well, only if it is done right. Banks have for year been telling customers how greatly valued they are. However when you go to a bank you see they have chained the pens to the counter. Employees will get used to monitoring provided it is explained and done openly.

3. A word about Employment Tribunals

The other day an employer mentioned to me that they had a lot of employment tribunal experience. The implication being that it held no fear for them. My experience has been that the tribunal will try its upmost to get the employer to settle the matter by making some form of payment. As a generalisation therefore it may be better to make a serious attempt to negotiate a settlement prior to incurring legal costs. However for those employers who are going to show their ex-employee who is boss (even after the employee has left the company) the tribunal offers a relatively cheap means of fighting it out and the issues normally in dispute do not use up company resources to the same extent as a civil trial. However look out for a pressure to settle the matter at the tribunal door.

The downside is that you will be playing out your moment of justice before a fairly unsympathetic audience of tribunal members.

Another drawback is some employers see the tribunal as a bit of a lottery. The cases sometimes seem to conflict:

- An employee downloaded pornography, had a brief interview and was sacked for gross misconduct.

  Held: Unfair as it was not investigated and the manager did not adhere to the company's code of conduct.

- Employee got stuck in a porn site. Interviewed and code of conduct referred to.

  Held: Dismissal fair.

- Employee had unauthorised access to wage data.

  Held: Dismissal fair. It would have been easier if the Company had a written security policy.

- A long standing employee hacked into a company database containing customer information, altering 90 secure passwords to do so. He did not do it for personal gain but to do his job more effectively.

Held: Unfair dismissal.

• Employee looked up travel companies to arrange a holiday.

Held: Dismissal fair.

• Company concerned about internet abuse by all employees compiled a list of offenders and categorised into Bad, very bad etc. Then dismissed those in bottom two categories.

Held: Fair.

The conclusions that I have made are:

1. In tribunals the procedure you adopt in investigating and deciding the conduct is very important. The "Off with his head" – knee-jerk reaction is not the preferred method.

2. Remember: evidence collected after the employee is dismissed will not be admitted in the tribunal even if it shows that you were right. This suggests collect the evidence first and then dismiss with firm reasons for doing so.

3. There are few sure winning cases.

THE INFORMATION
COMMISSIONER
GETS TOUGH

CHAPTER 5
THE DATA PROTECTION RACKET

When Scott McNealy, CEO Sun Microsystems said "You have zero privacy anyway. Get over it" he did not take into account the ingenuity of the European Union (EU). The EU is opposed to the McNealy approach.

The good news is that there is no shortage of information to assist you to understand the data protection law – and that is the bad news too.

The law is contained in the Data Protection Act 1998 ("DPA"). There are 4 codes to further explain the Act. It is expected that supplementary guidance documents will be produced such as the very helpful 30 page document on Monitoring and Surveillance. There is an overlap with the Regulation of Investigatory Powers Act 2000 ("RIPA") which in itself is not easy to follow.

Gerald Kaufmann MP when Chairing a Parliamentary Select Committee said that the DPA "is one of the most insane pieces of legislation ever to have passed through this house".

That is not to say it is not helpful. The legislation even has a slightly Bhuddist feel with its "Eight Principles" that enshrine the core values of the Act which focuses on how personal data must be "processed". The eight principles are that data must be:

1. fairly and lawfully processed;

2. any processing must be for limited purposes;

3. adequate, relevant and not excessive;

4. accurate and kept up to date;

5. not kept longer than is necessary;

6. processed in accordance with the data subject's rights;

7. secure against damage or loss; and

8. not transferred to countries outside EEA without adequate protection.

The Buddhist theme continues with the "six" conditions. Without at least one of these conditions data processing cannot take place:

1. consent of the "data subject";

2. necessary for the performance of a contract with the data subject;

3. necessary for compliance with a legal obligation;

4. protection of the vital interests of the data subject;

5. the administration of justice;

6. necessary for the purpose of the legitimate interests of the data controller.

Some critically say that the legislation alternates between statements of the obvious and a rubbish dump of detailed, sometimes conflicting, requirements. Comparisons have been made of the 100,000's of words on Data Protection and the fact that the Gettysburg Address was 267 words long.

However, data protection is here to stay. It was rolled out in the Data Protection Directive across the European Union. So the law is similar in each of the EU countries. The intrusive capability of computers and databases has caused the protection of privacy to be a serious business. IT Professionals can deal with it by keeping their heads down and hope that they are not caught. However this is not the recommended approach for IT Professionals. Alternatively they can get an understanding of the legislation and know how to find information. A further incentive to IT

Professionals is the personal criminal liability imposed by the Act for directors and managers for taking a casual attitude to compliance by "connivance" i.e. turning a blind eye.

The concept can no longer be viewed as "a new fangled idea" and the statement of the Information Commissioner (who polices the UK) to the effect that the Commission's approach is "no more Mr Nice guy" illustrates this. We can expect prosecutions to increase.

So how can the IT Professional get a grasp on the legislation and manage its requirements without intense study or continually calling in experts?

In four ways:

1. *By keeping in mind the basic intention of the legislation*

A business must look after personal data being information concerning a living person e.g. name, address, birthday, health, preferences etc. It is not to be kept longer that necessary, it must be accurate, audited, kept securely and if it is sensitive (e.g. medical records) a high standard of care is required. A company or organisation must register with the Information Commission: called "notification". One person is made responsible for it called the "Data Controller". There are common sense exceptions to this rule e.g. routine monitoring. The easiest way to deal with the information is to get the consent of the person to whom the information relates.

2. *By relying on the helpline*

The Commissioner's Office puts a lot of emphasis on being user-friendly. You can simply make a telephone call and ask for guidance. Such calls are anonymous. This has proved so popular that the line is sometimes engaged. On the record enquiries can be made by email and in writing.

The Information Commissioner's Office:

Information line: 01625 545745
To notify: 01625 545740
Switchboard: 01625 545700
www.informationcommissioner.gov.uk
data@dataprotection.gov.uk

3. *By understanding the risk*

The Commissioner tries to deal with matters by negotiation. If you demonstrate that you take the subject seriously and try to work with his office to resolve problems that arise it is unlikely that you will be prosecuted. Having said that in dealing with any data protection issues you should not make any admissions that may leave you open to prosecution. Such legislation requires scapegoats to be examples for others. As the Chinese say "kill the chicken to frighten the fox". The Commissioner must take prosecutions if the legislation is to have credibility. Sometimes the witnesses may be your own employees so prosecutions may be difficult to defend.

4. *By noting the following 10 issues which frequently arise as set out below*

10 Data Protection Issues

1. *Transfers of data internationally*

International transfer can be divided into two different categories. Transfer inside and outside the European Union (EU).

Transfers of data within the EU. Within the EU there is no problem in transferring data. The EU countries are all subject to the Data Protection Directive. In fact, Italy and France have higher standards of protection than the UK.

Transferring data outside EU? You cannot transfer to 3rd parties outside EU unless there are adequate protections of rights and freedoms of the individual in that country.

In practical terms the best way to do this is to enter into a contract which should include, instructions on what the overseas company can and cannot do, security measures, include a right to audit organisation for compliance. Fortunately, a model agreement can be found on the Commissioner's web site. All that you need to do is to have each of the overseas companies to which you wish to send personal data to sign a copy of this agreement and abide by the terms. In large organisations with many overseas offices receiving personal data may seem daunting. Overseas Country Managers may not see this as a priority. However spurred on by the threat of criminal personal liability you will endeavour to convince them.

Here are several points of information that may be useful in trying to convince the overseas country managers:

(a) The Commission does not impose high standards on overseas businesses but expects some common sense procedures to be in place in order to protect data.

(b) The overseas country managers may ask you if this is the only alternative. There are several others (which are not much use) and the following may help to demonstrate that you have left no stone unturned:

- Where the EU has made a finding that the country is compliant then this is conclusive and you can freely send data to the overseas country as if it was part of the UK. However few countries have such a finding (they are listed on the Commissioner's web site). At the date of writing this is not worth checking.

- You can undertake your own research to ensure that the country has adequate protection. As such research has been estimated to cost £5000 per country, it is impractical. For instance, Australia and Hong Kong probably do have sufficient legislative measures to protect data however you should have a contract to minimise the risk to your company and yourself.

- Safe Harbour Agreements. US companies can enter into the Safe Harbour program. Safe harbour demonstrates that the US business is compliant for the purpose of the UK legislation. Once the US business has entered this program then data can be freely sent by the UK to this business as if it were a UK business. Much has been said about Safe Harbour. However US businesses treat this program with suspicion and few have signed up. Signing up allows the US government to investigate the signatories and impose penalties for those not complying with the rules. At present, most US businesses prefer to avoid this obligation. A list of US businesses that have signed up to Safe Harbour is linked to the Commissioner's web site.

- There is the usual exception where the person ("data subject") has agreed to the transfer overseas. However where data is being transferred overseas the consent needs to be very clear e.g. "I am sending this data to a country which is not protected. Do you agree? Sign here". There are samples of wording on the Commissioner's web site.

Conclusion, a contract with the overseas 3rd party business is the best and in the circumstances, the easiest method of compliance.

3. Global transfer of address lists to other companies and within the group

Address lists are personal data and the most practical way to proceed is to enter into a contract with overseas companies as suggested above if you wish to transfer data outside the EU. The transfer of address lists is a common occurrence. The Commissioner has not given any particular guidance on this area.

4. What is the risk of criminal prosecution?

The Act provides for criminal liability including failure to register, unlawfully procuring information (either knowingly or recklessly) and for failing to comply with a notice from the Commissioner.

So far, most of the cases have been for failing to register the fact that you are dealing with personal data. The registration is a simple low cost procedure. There are presently a handful of criminal proceedings per year for offences other than failure to register. This will increase if the Commissioner wishes to demonstrate that the legislation has teeth, however due to the expense of litigation the number of prosecutions are unlikely to be significant.

Therefore, statistically the risk is low however that is probably not the correct way of looking at the risk. As the evidence to support any prosecution may come from your own staff the risk of a disgruntled (or otherwise) staff member blowing the whistle on your business is probably higher with Data Protection than with other regulations as it is so easy to prove. Think:

– You are either registered or not registered.

– You either have a corporate culture that cares about the use of data or doesn't care. Your employees can give evidence of your attitude. A cavalier attitude on the part of the IT Professional or management may just inflame the Commissioner enough to take action. The IT Professionals is in a position to influence this culture.

If you are prosecuted under the Data Protection legislation the penalty is a fine rather than imprisonment. The downside is a prosecution results in a criminal conviction.

5. *Policies and procedures*

It is important to have written policies and procedures relating to Data Protection in order to protect the company from the actions of its employees.

The best way to illustrate the importance of policies and procedures covering Data Protection use can be seen in the Commissioner's ruling in a case involving a building society. A mother went with her child into a building society. It seemed to the building society's teller that the woman was unreasonably scolding her child and became concerned for the child's welfare. The teller served the mother and then using the details of name, address etc. from the mother's passbook she called the social services and reported the conduct of the mother.

The social services acted upon the information and visited the mother. The mother, naturally, was angry at the Building Society and reported the incident to the Commissioner. The Commissioner decided that there was misuse of information by the teller and she was liable. However the building society were not liable, as they has specifically forbidden such behaviour in their policies and procedures.

As previously noted, the policies must be communicated to staff.

6. *Have a Data Protection Notice*

This is notice given to customers when collecting data outlining the use to which data is to be put. They can be seen on the bottom of forms. If you do not have such a notice then it is likely that you can only use the data collected for purposes which are very obvious. One solicitor's firm have gone as far to put such a notice on its business cards so that the information obtained on the business cards acquired in the exchange can be processed.

The notice has to be fairly specific. However as more restrictions are placed on the collection of data it will be possible to qualify data in such a way as to make it valuable. When collecting data if you ask a non-customer "Can we advise you of new products?". Then that allows you to add that person to your mailing list when advising potential customers of new products. Failure to ask such questions when you collect a person's name and address will mean that you have the data but cannot let them know about your new products.

7. *Have a privacy statement*

This is a company statement on how the company uses data in general. This can frequently be seen as a link at the bottom of the web page. This may offer no legal protection in itself although it does demonstrate the commitment of a business to protect the data of its employees and third parties. Since other companies increasingly have such a notice then it may be best to have one.

8. *Data passing through the UK in transit*

The Commissioner has stated that information passing through the UK in transit is not a transfer of data for the purpose of the Act and it does not apply.

However as businesses become more global and the flow of data may be partly outside the UK even in routine transactions, the question of where the data can be accessed gains importance.

As always, the IT Professional may be called upon to account for data being put at risk. The IT Professional should be aware of the path of the data flows within his organisation.

In some cases it may be best to encrypt sensitive personal data.

9. *Subject Data Access Request*

This is an important subject for the IT Professional and is dealt with fully in Part 4: Emergency Situations below.

10. *Jurisdiction*

Generally, the Information Commission's jurisdiction only covers acts committed in the UK. Therefore if the misuse occurs outside the UK then the UK data controller is not responsible.

The Information Commissioner has indicated that the Act applies where the server is in UK even though the data is in effect foreign e.g. emails of French employees processed by an UK server.

The general rule is that if data is downloaded in the UK then it is subject to the Act. An exception to this is if it was in transit only.

Subjects such as Data Protection do seem to attract a fair share of po-faced, section quoting zealots. However these individuals should not dissuade the prudent IT Professional from supporting the principles of data protection. The risks of failing to do so both for the business and for the IT Professional are not worth it.

ENFORCING CONFIDENTIALITY
AT WORK

CHAPTER 6
PROTECTION BY CONTRACT

Businesses can try to protect their industry secrets by confidentiality agreements and by trying to restrict the future employment of employees.

Confidentiality Agreements

The good news is that you do not need a confidentiality agreement to impose a duty of confidentiality on your employees. If an employee leaves you then there is an unwritten *implied* duty for him to keep things secret after he leaves as well as when he is in your employment. The law expects employees to be dutiful (the legal expression for this type of law until not too long ago was Master and Servant). Employees are in a position of trust they should not abuse this position by revealing the employer's business to people outside the business.

However what an employer regards as confidential information may not be the same view as the courts, which tend to lean on the side of the employee and give a narrow interpretation to this right of the employer.

Most employment contracts have a written term binding the employee to confidentiality. Businesses which need to tell others about products or services which are still under development, usually get that person to sign a confidentiality agreement. People selling a business or offering confidential know how get a confidentiality agreement signed.

So how good is an unwritten implied duty not to tell?

Consultants and employees too often walk out of their employer's offices with (for example) the source code of a successful computer program or other secrets. It is when they start their own business on the strength of it that the trouble starts.

The law here is fairly certain. These types of actions are very common in the lower courts as jilted former employers pursue renegade former employees. Such former employees are financially strapped after investing in their own businesses using the know-how gained at their former employer's expense.

When considering if the information was confidential the courts will apply a three point test:

1. *Was there a quality of confidentiality about the information?* For instance it was the company strategy in relation to their competitors or pricing.

2. *Was it given in circumstances which suggested it was confidential?* Some go further and apply a trade secrets colour coding and register books of information in a special store. Many companies mark documents as "confidential". Employees tend to work against this system by marking their every run of the mill Powerpoint demonstration and other document confidential. So some control needs to be exercised over these terms.

3. *Was it used to the detriment of the giver?* For instance, did the employee start selling the same products or know-how to the same customers?

Lists of customers are usually protected. Cases often turn on the credibility of the witnesses and you can end up being declared a liar if the judge doesn't believe you. On the positive side this fate awaits your opponent too.

Restrictive covenants in employment/consultancy contracts

A traitor leaving the company causes heightened emotions. Much money has been thrown away on disputes arising from this issue.

– Employers be warned that if your initial bluff of threatening to sue your former employees should they dare to go near one of your existing clients does not work, it may be better to accept it and move on.

– Former employees be warned that just because your lawyer tells you the employer probably will lose, this does not stop irate employers irrationally pursuing you and wasting a lot of your time and money as well as their own.

When a "traitor" leaves the company all hands reach for the employment contract. There you will find the "restrictive covenant". This is intended to stop a departing employee competing, or walking off with the employer's clients. Such covenants are interpreted against the employer so such covenants need to have been drafted carefully to ensure they work.

Restrictive covenants are often copies from some other employment contract without much thought by the employer. However the more attractive the client or the money to be made in competing the more likely the covenant is to be tested and found wanting.

There are no special issues for IT in this area of the law however the IT industry has been caught up in many disputes due to the value of the innovations and importance to the business of the departing employee.

Here are 10 points for the IT Professional to bear in mind:

1. The covenant must be reasonable and protect the employer's business interests. The test of "reasonableness" will be at the time the covenant is applied. Therefore if your business has changed making the form of covenant used redundant by the time the man walks out, "tough". Unless you have changed the covenant during his employment.

2. The "business interests" of a company means "keeping customers", "keeping its workforce" and keeping "confidential information" (see *confidential information*).

3. You cannot stop an employee taking his general know how elsewhere. But something special e.g. the Coca Cola® formula would be protected.

4. You can't protect your "business interests" in relation to that employee forever. There should be a time limit in the agreement for example 6 months. If you do not voluntarily put in a time limit the court will not put in one for you. The court will simply find the condition too onerous and throw it out. So do not ask for too much in your agreement or you may end up getting nothing.

5. It must be limited to the type of business in which the employee is involved. The restrictive covenant cannot cover all the different areas in which a company is involved if the employee only knows about one of those areas. So too, the employee must have had significant contact with any clients covered by the agreement.

6. It cannot cover the entire world. It should be limited to a geographical location. In the days of the world wide web this may be difficult to define but remember any uncertainty is probably going to be interpreted in favour of your hated former employee.

7. If the former employee's skills cannot be used for anything else he has a good argument not to be bound by the covenant.

8. You may opt for a term that the employee is not to solicit any of the businesses customers, this may cause the employee to pause before he begins to contact his former customers. However it is almost impossible for an employer to police.

9. Courts will generally allow an employer a little time to settle his clients down after a defection: then rule that the employer is on his own and needs to compete.

10. Very junior or casual staff – not much chance of a covenant sticking.

Do not let me dissuade employers from imposing such covenants. But I do not want to raise expectations too high. In the case of important employees who can do your business a lot of damage it is important to consult an IT solicitor.

PART 3
THE PRACTICAL LEGAL ISSUES

THE LICENCE READING
ROOM IN HELL

CHAPTER 7
LICENSING – ALL YOU NEED TO KNOW

The Basic Facts of Licensing

I assume that you may not like licences very much. Have you ever read a licence? If not go to Appendix 1. Assuming that you did go to Appendix 1 and followed the simple instruction "Read", you have just read a software licence. It is quite short isn't it? And considering it is a legal document, it is quite easy to follow. In effect, there is only one answer to nearly all questions concerning licences and that is "read the licence". Remember this before you pick up the phone to your in-house lawyer or even more so, a private practice lawyer, and it will save you a lot of time and money. Also they are probably going to ask you what does it say or to send over a copy of the licence so that they can read it.

Licences do follow a basic format but sometimes they are not so easy to read as the example in Appendix 1. For instance the Microsoft® eOpen License Agreement v.6.1 ("Open licence") which I do not attach in order not to dampen your enthusiasm. That license is an umbrella licence: it sets out the general terms applicable to the many Microsoft products that you are authorised to use under this type of licence. Then it refers to "Product Use Rights" which is a separate document setting out the terms for individual products. I hope the Microsoft lawyers will not be offended if I say that the best thing about this licence is that, in the circumstances, it is mercifully short. I doubt if the lawyers went out of their way to make this difficult to read. They faced a complex situation. The twists and turns result from the lawyers trying to avoid problems and legally this may be as short as that licence gets.

Just remember the answer to all licensing questions is to "read the licence" so if you are working with the Open licence you now know what you should do with it.

Principles of licensing

1. The owner of a computer program has rights which can stop others using the program. These are powerful and protected by the criminal and civil law in copyright and trademark. The owner can only sell the program once, just like you would sell a bicycle or any other commodity once only. However the owner wants to be paid everytime somebody obtains a copy. This process of giving people permission to use a copy of a program is called a "licence". It is a contract between the software publisher ("the Licensor") and the licence user ("the Licensee").

2. If you are buying a software program which is for the use of your company alone you may be able to buy it outright. This is called an "assignment". If the owner assigns you the rights then you own the software and you can do any thing you want with it for example you can sell licenses to use it. However in most cases an owner of a program will grant you a licence to use it. This will enable the owner to grant other people a licence to use the program as well and therefore gain more money.

3. A licence does not need to be in writing and it is possible to prove that you were granted a licence by the surrounding circumstances. This is called an implied licence. However in the circumstances of a verbal licence it would be very difficult to prove the terms of the licence.

4. It could be argued that the written licence is for the benefit of both seller and buyer. However in reality although it does tell the licensee how to utilize the software it also tends to impose restrictions on use, liability etc., which are in favour of the software publisher.

5. Should there be a standard licence? Clearly, yes. However there are many ways for a software publisher to sell and allow use of its products, depending in some part on the bargaining position

of the parties. For the most part we tend not to read the licence and in mass market products this system works. However not to read a contract from a smaller supplier especially, when services are being provided is reckless. It is no excuse to say that you did not read the contract. In my experience those contracts heavily favour the software publisher (see *Computer Services — what if it all goes wrong?* (below)).

The standard licence and the four main formats of software licence

The following are a good place to start:

1. Standard licence

This licence exists only in the mind of the software salesman when you enquire what type of licence you are getting. When you are dealing with off-the-shelf relatively cheap software products then you probably do not care much about the terms. However if you have a lot of money riding on the software you must exercise caution when you are presented with what appears to be a Standard Licence Agreement. These may be neatly printed and graphically supported and give every appearance of being the "standard terms" however, they usually contain terms that are against your interest. The more money you are paying the more carefully these should be read. If the licence is going to be at the centre of your business, for example software like CRM, then get a lawyer to review it.

2. Bespoke licence

These are when the licence is made from scratch to fit the specific software and/or services. Here what you are getting for your money and who carries the can when it goes wrong is of such importance that the involvement of a lawyer is recommended.

3. Shrinkwrap licence

This is contained inside the plastic shrink wrapped box containing the software. The idea behind this is that by breaking the seal (pulling off the shrinkwrap) you agree to the terms of the licence.

This is an attempt to try and fit software sales into standard contract law. The terms of a contract must be communicated to the customer otherwise lawyers would argue that they are not binding. The opening of the shrinkwrap confirms that the customer accepts the terms of the licence.

There is great doubt that this method works. As you have read, the terms of a contract must be communicated to the buyer. In this case that means brought to the attention of the end user licensee before the contract is made. It seems that on the opening of the box it is too late to satisfy that requirement. The software vendors sometimes offer some extra benefit such as website support in exchange for agreeing to the terms of the licence. This may work. However it is always worth considering how you got notice of the terms of the contract and arguing that the terms were not communicated to you in time. It is worth doing this if you are trying to avoid any contractual term.

4. Clickwrap licence

You will usually see this licence when you load a new program. When installing often the first screen that you see contains the terms of the licence. You scroll down the terms (for most people very quickly) and then you get the option of clicking a button saying "I accept the terms" or "I do not accept the terms". If you choose the latter you cannot get into the program. No doubt you can return it and get your money back. However, most people hit the "I accept" button. Hence the name "clickwrap". Legally, this click has significance because whereas the person who tears off the shrinkwrap may argue ignorance, the person who gets the chance to read the terms even though he may not do so is caught by those terms. In the same way as a person who signs a document even though he hasn't read it he is bound by that document.

Consumers get a little more leeway if the small print is unreasonable. But not so much that you can continue not reading anything. You may say, "But so what, no one is going to find out that you are using infringing software." This is not quite so. Your employees may know especially if they are in your IT Department and they may blow the whistle on you (see *Whistleblowing*).

Most downloads of software from the internet have a clickwrap type agreement at the start of any download. Say you do not accept and you do not get to download.

Twelve types of software licence

One reason that there is no such thing as a standard software licence is that there are many ways that software publishers choose to sell their products. The software being supplied often does not change but the method of determining the price differs with the benefits derived from use.

The more cynical would say the price is what the software publishers can get away with. The ultimate software agreement may be where the customer is faced with such a complicated and involved calculation he just reaches for his cheque book and pays rather than arguing. This could be described as bluff ware. However in reality in buying software you may be just as anxious to impose limits on your company's use of the software in order to get a cheaper deal. There are many variations of these limitations. The limitations range from being limited to a named person or a particular computer, a building or site.

Common consumer and small business licences

1. *Single user licence-computer*

This is the most common licence used by consumers and business. It means that you have a licence for one computer. Anyone can use the software program but it must only be used on that one computer. If you want to use the program on more that one computer then you must buy a licence for each computer. Anyone buying a Dell® computer will be familiar with this type of licence.

Can you transfer this licence to another computer? I would say no, but read the licence.

What if your computer shuts down and stops working surely you can transfer the software then? I would say no, but read the licence. Apart from the licence you may have a claim against the supplier if the machine was not fit for the purpose.

2. *Single user licence – individual*

This would allow one named person to use the software on whichever machine it is installed. It is best for businesses to avoid this arrangement as personnel change and the licence that your company purchased may walk out the door when the employee leaves the company.

3. *Program suite licence*

What happens when there is a software product which allows use of more than one program e.g. Microsoft® Office. The licence terms stop the use of the applications separately. So you cannot use Microsoft Word on one machine and Microsoft Excel on another.

Common Business Licences

These so called "volume licencing arrangements" allow customers to get a substantial discount on the software purchased. This is how companies which are over 5 users buy software in common use in their organsations. Some of these agreements are written in such a way that it is almost impossible to understand. So do not think it is just you.

The downside of getting these substantial discounts is that the licences tie your business into using the volume software rather than having the flexibility of using software from many different suppliers. This gives the software publisher the upper hand and if the relationship goes sour can leave your company vulnerable. There is no such thing as a free lunch. Make sure your Finance Director realises that when he chooses the cheapest option.

4. *Network licence*

This simply allows use of a software program for all those connected to one server or one Local Area Network (LAN).

5. *Concurrent Use Licence*

Here the access to the software of those connected to the network is limited to a certain number of users at any one time. If there are 100 people using the network and the concurrent licence provides for 10 concurrent users at anyone time then if 11 people want to use the application on the network one will need to wait until a place becomes available. Most companies using this type of licence have purchased spare capacity.

6. *Site Licence*

This is where anyone in one building or office or place can have access to the software.

7. *Enterprise licence*

This is where the whole business has a licence to use the software. This is useful where there are many offices, some overseas. In some cases there may be separate companies included which are part of the same group.

The important thing to remember is when deciding on which software to buy nothing is written in stone. There are many ways to buy. Once the software is written there is no increase in cost if the software is provided to 100 people rather than 110 people or 100 sites rather than 10 sites. In a takeover situation it is worth speaking to the software publisher to see if any savings can be made. This is best done before the purchase as there is a form of licence called stiff ware. This is where the buyer tries to negotiate with a software publisher after a merger. The terms of the original licence may not allow the software to be used by the new company. Therefore the purchaser must buy the software again (see *Mergers and Acquisitions: Check Out that Software Title* below).

8. *Client/server licence*

This is where the software is placed on the server however most of the processing is done on the users' computers eg. accounting software.

The Internet: free for all licences?

When downloading software from the internet "free" may not be necessarily free. If you download something and then do not abide by the licence terms you may be opening your company, you (and even worse your boss) up to civil or criminal liability.

Lawyers have been hard at work to put the more unconventional "untamed" software into defined boxes. So sadly software distribution on the internet is not as wild and crazy as it once was.

Here are a few of the common licences and terminology:

9. *Shareware licence*

Is this free? Well yes and no. This is the name given to software that you download for a trial period e.g. 30 days and then delete if you do not like it. It is becoming a very common way to sell software. However there is a downside in that people do not delete the software after use they just leave it cluttering up their hard drives. If you are raided then keeping this on your computer is a civil and criminal offence once the expiry date is up (see *Copyright infringement* below).

Shareware may sound casual however there is an Association of Shareware Professionals imposing certain standards on such software.

10. *Freeware licence*

Is this free? Well yes and no. It does not cost money but it is usually subject to restriction. Otherwise why would the software publisher have a licence. There is a General Public Licence (*www.gnu.org*) which is popular for this type of software. If you produce software and were happy for people to use it at no charge you would be upset if someone took it and started to sell it, so you would stop this wouldn't you? How? Well the only way to stop this behaviour is to insist that the user abides by the terms of a licence.

11. *Public Domain Software Licence*

Is the free? Yes. No restrictions are allowed. The software publisher has put this up on the internet and stated that he will not enforce his rights.

What happens if a software publisher who places his software in the Public Domain changes his mind? One thing is that any person using the software relying on the statement that he will not enforce his rights will be able to rely on this permission especially if they have done something to their detriment as a result of this promise. If he did change his mind he would need to create a licence setting out the new terms. However if he ever tried to enforce the licence he would probably be met by the defence that the user thought it was a Public Domain Licence. Therefore he would probably try to get evidence that users knew the terms had changed. For instance proving the software in use had a clickware licence.

12. *Open Source Software Licence*

Linux is the best example of this. The source code is made available to all without restriction. A team of programmers continue to give their time at no charge to improve the source code. Contributions to the improvement of the basic code are made by universities, businesses and government. The source code can be taken and modified and sold commercially.

If you are in charge of the software being used in your company assume that every bit of software or .exe file is the subject of some sort of restriction or cost. If it is on your computer network then you may be liable for it.

TEN HANDY TIPS FOR INSTRUCTING AN OUTSOURCING LAWYER

CHAPTER 8
DANGEROUS GROUND
FOR IT PROFESSIONALS
– THE CHALLENGING SITUATIONS

There are three legal issues that will arise for the IT Professional that he should treat with caution:

- when software contracts go wrong

- negotiating a software contract

- mergers and acquisitions.

Software Contracts – what if it all goes wrong?

The problem

Too often, the installation of a computer system usually ends up with some sort of falling out.

A typical situation falls into six stages:

1. The computer supplier makes valiant efforts to give you the fantastic system that he promised.

2. The supplier finds himself putting far more man hours and resources into your job than he had estimated.

3. Slowly your employees are putting up with some very odd ways of manipulating data: it emerges that things that could have been achieved with a few strokes under the old

discredited system takes many key stokes and in an order that you are assured that you will get used to.

4. Your employees fall into two camps: those who wait patiently for bugs to be fixed and those who build lists. Discontent will rise and a feeling grows that maybe the old computer system that everyone complained about was not so bad after all. As you did not want to let go of it in the first place you will feel vindicated.

5. Ironically as the frustration of staff members builds the Computer Supplier will slump into depression and turn up less and less at your premises.

6. At some stage you must face the fact that you have been sold a pup and the supplier who you so painstakingly chose discredited: the project which was hailed by the director in charge of IT as "the winter of the firm's discontent" is in tatters.

The solution

Your job may be on the line. Let's hope that it was penny pinching by the Finance Director and you were not responsible for the cheaper option.

The first thing to do when you are in a hole like this is stop digging and follow the following 5 Point Game plan:

1. Come clean with management. This is everyone's problem. Start to document the errors. Keep a file.

2. When you tell the management their impulse may be to give this supplier their marching orders and get in someone else. A recommendation from a software publisher such as IBM® for a team to put it right. You should hesitate here. Imagine if you had supplied a system which was not doing what it was supposed to do. You would try your best and put extra help in to solve the problem. Then you would start to feel a little depressed and not turn up so much. You would find the additional help is wanted for more successful projects that you have on the go. You would start turning up less and less

to the problem project. If the buyer finally lost patience and sacked you and got in someone else to complete the project what a huge relief this would be for you. The sacking would be a great face-saving chance for you to say that they did not give you enough time or enough of a chance. Assuming that you had received most of the money you would be as "happy as Larry" to be sent packing ready to inflict your services with hopefully more luck this time on another company. In fact you would assume the moral high ground even if you have left the buyer in the lurch.

3. Do not let the supplier off the hook by sending him packing. A better way to proceed is meet with the supplier to see if he agrees that the contract is not going according to plan. Document how bad he thinks it is going. Then ask how he intends to keep up his side of the contract, give him a chance to put it right. At the same time you may want to get in a new team to find out from you point of view how hard it will be to put right. Confirm that meeting in writing.

4. Once the report of the independent consultant is back you can decide how to proceed.

5. You must bear in mind that having spent far more hours on the contract than he intended the supplier may have a claim against you for the extra time. Whether or not he may have a claim against you and whether he has given you some benefit or he has made a complete mess of it and you have a claim against him, you need to negotiate a settlement to bring the matter to an end:

    a) Ensuring that you get an assignment of any software that he is leaving behind and that you believe you may use in the future. Failing that a licence to use it as much as you want.

    b) That he agrees not make any claim against you. In exchange you should promise not to make any claim against him.

    c) Any other benefit that you can get away with.

I suggest that you enter into this settlement while he is feeling vulnerable as a result of the mess that he is leaving behind and he has the potential of a claim from you. To let this matter hang is to risk being left using part of a system where you do not have a transfer of the IP rights. That could cause all sorts of problems. Again, get a lawyer's advice on the wording of the settlement agreement. You do not want to leave any loose ends.

But what about the contract?

Before starting the 5 point game plan you must get the contract out of the draw and read it (maybe for the first time). If there is no formal contract document then you must ask yourself if there is any binding agreement between you and the supplier.

Too often the supply of software systems goes forward without a contract being signed. Like a marriage the parties are full of good intentions even though the divorce rate is very high. Sometimes when dealing with one man bands or the smaller suppliers of software, there is no contract.

In other companies a draft contract is prepared but through a combination of a slow legal process and the project taking off regardless, the contract is never finalised or signed. This may be hard to believe, however, you can imagine in agreements between a large supplier and large end user the contract must laboriously ping pong between the respective legal departments. Meanwhile the project managers just want to get on with it.

There are two situations:

a)   No contract at all or where there is no signed final contract.

What happens when the contract is not signed? Well like any salesman once the job is underway the supplier usually believes the buyer is committed. In fact many suppliers may feel this is a useful tactic. However as you know, if no contract has been entered into then there is no meeting of minds. Technically the buyer can simply walk away as he has not entered into a contract and therefore is under no legal duty to do anything. In some cases the courts have allowed the buyer to do just that – walk away.

However in other cases the buyer has been made to pay for the value received. Which seems a fairer approach (depending on the facts).

The main disadvantage for the seller in having no written contract is that there will be no exclusion of liability clause to provide protection (see below).

The main disadvantage for the buyer is that the seller will say that what has been supplied was what was promised whereas the buyer will point to all the things they were told or thought they were getting. Goal posts are moved and memories become selective.

Go straight for the 5 Point Game Plan

b) Where there is a contract

The situation is different when there is a formal contract. Get that contract out of the draw and, yes, read it. Did you instruct solicitors to review the contract for you before you entered into the agreement? Of course you didn't – you hate solicitors. No, well you are not alone in making that mistake: it is very common.

Fighting the exclusion clause

If there is a formal contract then you may be in trouble as it will contain an exclusion clause limiting the liability of the supplier. It will probably be very wide so that whatever the supplier has done you are not allowed to make any claim (see *Negotiating a Software Contract*). But can the software supplier selling a system with services really get away with providing bad service Scot Free? Well yes and no. In this book you will see that if you signed the agreement a deal is a deal however stupid you have been. However as always in the law nothing is black and white. The courts do not like to support companies who sell rubbish and then hide behind the small print of the contract terms.

Exclusion clauses are construed by the courts against the party relying on them. This is a plus for the buyer and means that the supplier must get it right or a court may strike it out.

Here are three points to use:

1. *The Sale of Goods argument*

- The Sale of Goods Act 1979 ("the SOG") provides that goods must be of satisfactory quality and fit for the purpose. Also if you tell the supplier that you want to use the goods in a certain way and it is reasonable for you to rely on a seller's knowledge then the goods must come up to that standard.

- However if you are a business (rather than a consumer) then these implied conditions can be excluded. In a supplier's contract it is likely that the SOG will be excluded and then you will be back to square one. However suppliers make mistakes in contracts too. Some suppliers do not get a lawyer's advice and fail to exclude the SOG. This can happen to a US company which uses the US version of the contract.

- So what is reasonable? Very difficult but here is a flavour of the potential variables:

  strength of the bargaining positions of the parties, was it a "take it or leave it" situation, was the buyer likely to be aware of the condition, was it common in the trade, would the seller really be expected to meet the liability or could the buyer easily insure?

  For example, where a seller tries to say that "if you do not report the defect within seven days in writing, then we are not liable" that would probably be going too far if the breach was serious.

- Here is a flavour of the counter arguments that the supplier may use (all used in past court cases):

  - The Sale of Goods Act protects goods and not services such as systems support (this argument seems to run and run).

- Software is licensed and not sold it is not goods (seems logical but the courts will try and help the buyer).

- The person who negotiated the deal was senior and expert enough to understand it.

- There was price reduction as it was a buyer's market.

- Does the company place the condition in its own standard terms? If so then it understood it.

- Has it been amended in negotiation?

- Another example would be a substantial contract where the parties have equal bargaining power. They are the best judges of what is commercially fair. Unless the court can be sure that one party has taken advantage of the other or that the term is so unreasonable that it could not have been understood or considered then it will leave the deal to the parties making it.

- If you succeed in the SOG argument it would allow you to reject the goods and threaten to sue for any damage caused to you.

2. *Liability for personal injury and death cannot be excluded*

3. *You cannot be sold the Brooklyn Bridge. If the seller sells you software rights which he does not own then you are entitled to get your money back*

Finally, when considering court action please bear in mind that damages are generally to put you back in the situation that you would have been in if the contract had not been made. They are not to punish the defendant however duff a job he has done.

Negotiating a Contract for the Supply of Software

You are at the stage of buying the CRM system. The supplier has prepared a fairly lengthy report and spent quite a lot of time at your company already to assess the situation and estimate the cost of the system and accompanying services.

You want to go ahead and the supplier gives you a draft contract for you to review and sign. What do you do with that draft contract? You read it and give it to a solicitor who specialises in reviewing software contracts.

Safe that the matter is in the hands of your solicitor here are six points on matters that you will wish to know about before you enter into the contract:

1. *The exclusion clause*

Somewhere in the contract you will find the exclusion clause. This limits the liability of the supplier. Software suppliers tend to exclude liability for as much as they can.

A common limitation is to cap the amount of any claim that you may make in court to be no more that the price that you paid for the software. This can leave the buyer very out of pocket.

The consequences of defective software are not limited to the cost of the software but can cause severe damage to the rest of the business causing the claim price to be far higher than the price of the software. If the price is only a few thousand then it is probably reasonable to limit liabilty as no one would expect them to risk a multi-million lawsuit for such a small reward. However the cost of a contract supplying a CRM with services is an expensive proposition.

2. *Damages*

What is the amount of damages (compensation) you will get if the contract goes wrong?

The type of compensation that you can get will be expressed in the contract using the terms "direct" losses and "consequential" losses:

- *"Direct" losses*. These are losses which directly and naturally flow from the breach of contact. They are the price paid, cost of putting it right, any reasonably incurred emergency short term fixes and direct lost profits.

- *"Consequential" losses*. These are indirect losses which do not directly and naturally flow from the breach of contact. These include lost profits which do not directly and naturally flow from the breach. They should not be too remote.

This is a complicated area of law and what you need to know is – don't allow the supplier to exclude direct losses but expect the supplier to exclude consequential loss.

3. Can you transfer it?

Can you let another company use the software? Can you sell your rights in it to another company? The software supplier should give a licence to act as freely as your business requires in using the software.

4. Who is going to use the software? Make sure it is the right company/employee

This is a matter if reading the licence and ensuring that the type of licence is appropriate for the requirements of your business (see *Licensing – the basics* at page 73 above).

5. Escrow agreement

What happens if the software vendor becomes insolvent or is unable or unwilling to keep up with commitments? Then the buyer will need to get access to the software to keep the system up to remedy errors and keep the system up to date. This is usually achieved by an escrow agreement. Here the source code is held by a third party and released to the buyer on specified events such as insolvency or failure to support. The terms are fairly standard and a body such as the National Computing Centre produces standard terms and will accept deposits.

6. *Termination*

You do not want the supplier to terminate the contract because you have breached an important condition such as your failure to make an interim payment. However if things are going wrong then you will be reluctant to continue paying the supplier until he puts things right. But if you do not hand over the money the supplier will tell you not to use the system until the instalment is paid. If you cannot use the software your business could suffer.

It is best not to leave a consideration of these issues until the problem arises. The contract will deal with what happens on termination or if the matter is going badly wrong.

Mergers and acquisitions

When a company buys your business they want to know what they are getting. This check of the business assets is called due diligence. Part of the assets to be checked is the ownership of software.

The buyer company does not physically check everything it relies on warranties. These are personal promises usually by the directors that everything is in order. So during a sale a director will ask the IT Professional "We are software compliant, aren't we?". Too often the answer may be "Yes" but in reality it is "I haven't got a clue". For a more detailed discussion of this see *Compliance* at page 73.

A problem for the seller company is that directors are personally liable. Also the company is giving all the evidence of non-compliance to the buying company. This could be used against them in any action or prosecution.

The problem for the buyer company is that suing on the warranty costs money – it is better to get it right in the first place.

In many transactions the lawyers either focus on the key IP issues and therefore the software is left for the incoming IT Professional to sort out. This means that during the period it takes to appraise and remedy the situation he has to work in a non-compliant environment. The IT Professional will be expected to adopt the attitude that "the show must go on". However this may attach a civil and the criminal law for both the IT Professional and the directors who turn a blind eye.

Often there is no time to sort matters out before completion. The purchase can be scheduled to complete two months after the agreement is made. To check all the assets may be a task that requires over six months therefore completion takes place and the due diligence process continues after the sale.

IT Professionals must accept the reality that in a fast moving sale worth multi-millions, software compliance may be low down on the priority list of the directors and lawyers.

As General Counsel of FAST, I had a call from a company which had taken over another company which owned software worth £400,000. After the takeover they were contacted by the software publisher (a large US multi-national) as they were using the software inconsistently with the licence. The bill came to £400K. The IT Professional blamed the software publisher. Maybe in that case it was the lawyers who overlooked the term. A disconnection between the lawyers and the IT Department needs to be avoided.

The solution for the IT Professional is to plan ahead and manage the IT environment and become software compliant to reduce their liability on a quick sale of a company's assets. Joining a software compliance program such as the one offered by FAST is a good option (see *Compliance* at page 130 below).

INTERNET INVESTIGATORS
A RARE BREED

CHAPTER 9
THE INTERNET

The internet allows even the smallest business to have their mistakes magnified into the monumental class.

For the most part the existing law can deal with the problems which arise on the internet.

Here are 6 internet issues of which the IT Professional should have some basic awareness.

1. Websites – 2 problems

IT Professionals can encounter problems in web commerce and use of trademarks on web sites.

Selling goods on your website – getting the price wrong

If you are selling goods on your website and you get the price wrong and someone buys the item for a substantial reduction then the law will come down in favour of the buyer. A deal is a deal – especially if it is a consumer. It is never a good idea to upset your customers by welching on a deal.

If you have been careless more than once then the Trading Standards offices could consider a prosecution under the Consumer Protection Act 1987.

But what happens if the mistake is such that you cannot be generous and put it down to experience? In that case you must argue it out with the customer and get the best deal you can.

Here are several ways to get out of this hole:

- Look at the terms and conditions for purchasing goods from the website. Is there anything there to tell the customer that the price may change or reserving the right to substitute the correct price in the event of error? If there is you are home dry (depending if you have sent the goods out). If you have already sent the goods out then possession really is 9/10th of the law and you are in for an uphill struggle. If there are no terms and conditions, you had better get some.

- Did the customer know that you had made a mistake? Now it may be obvious from the price or from the number of goods that the buyer had ordered that he knew and was taking advantage of your mistake.

  - Although the civil law says a deal is a deal there are exceptions. It provides that if the person knew the website operator had made a mistake then they cannot benefit from that mistake and you can set the contract aside.

  - A more forceful argument may be in the criminal law because the Theft Act provides that obtaining property by another's mistake is an offence. If you have sent the goods out then you may need to go down to the police station to take advantage of this option. Unlike the Copyright legislation the police are very familiar with the Theft Act and you can expect action. Even if you have not sent the goods out you can still argue that the buyer had made an attempt to obtain property by your mistake. Hopefully this will be used sparingly especially against potential customers and reserved for those who are taking a real liberty and will not let go.

If all else fails expect to be sued and remember that the County Court offers a fairly easy small claims procedure in straightforward cases where a deal is a deal.

Trademarks

It is wrong for a competitor to use your trademark in their website text or in their metatags to draw your customers to their site. Your first reaction will be to strangle your opposition and you may find this the cheapest and most effective remedy. The first step is to take an image of the screen (to use as evidence in case there is denial or to demonstrate the honesty of your competitor in future disputes). It may be something that can be dealt with by a telephone call, email or letter. You can do this or to be safe your solicitor can do it. It is tempting when you have got your competitor over a barrel to want to sue the pants off him (see that section in this book). However if he is the sort of competitor who is likely to dig his heels in then you are in dangerous territory as to get the court to make a quick order to stop the use of your trade mark involves injunctions and expensive legal moves. However you will get the satisfaction of knowing that your competitor's legal costs will be astronomic too – so if money is no object then go for it.

2. Dealing with laws in other countries

Choice of law/jurisdiction is one of the most complicated areas of law.

However for those dealing in ebusiness, where you have many such transactions or the loss is too much to bear here are eight simple guidelines:

a. The basic question is where was the contract made? In practice this would probably be the country of the supplier. However you can expect a counter argument that the contract should be subject to the laws of the country where the substantiality of the case occurred.

Specify in the contract that it is subject to the law of a certain jurisdiction. This should work in most business deals. You may be reluctant to submit to a US jurisdiction where damages and costs are likely to be that much higher.

b. A consumer is always going to be allowed to have the case tried in courts in their own country of residence whatever you say in the contract.

c. If you have physically injured someone then the victim will probably be allowed to decide on the jurisdiction.

d. Don't get into a position where one nation's courts are trying a case using the laws of another nation. For instance, a French court applying English laws. It is better to take your chances with a French Court deciding French law to avoid greater costs and possibly an unexpected result. The costs will increase if for instance the French Court calls upon experts to advise on English law (which they will do). An unexpected result may occur as the French judges are not used to applying English laws. I am sure that the English judges would be the first to admit that they have enough trouble applying English law (especially with the many EU and Government initiatives). IT Professionals are not the only people straining under this onslaught.

e. IP lawyers have been dealing with the problem of multi-jurisdictions for some time however IP cases are assisted by the international conventions which make the law fairly similar in all jurisdictions.

f. Criminal prosecutions will be within the country where the offence occurred. If there is a defendant who is resident in a foreign country in serious cases he can be extradited but otherwise he is beyond the jurisdiction. There could be a conviction in the absence of the defendant but this would be unusual.

g. In defamation proceedings relating to comments made on an internet site the claimant may try to pick the best country to take the proceedings. Words on the internet are published in effect to the whole world. For instance, in Finland they have a criminal defamation law which may be attractive for an injured claimant. The US may allow people greater freedom of expression than say the UK therefore a claimant may see England as a better and cheaper jurisdiction to launch a claim.

h.   In IP you may be using a name which in one country belongs
     to you but in other countries belongs to another company. In
     theory you could be sued in many different countries. However
     the courts in order to avoid this have begun to apply a test of
     targeting. So if you target a particular country with your product
     using a name which belongs to another company in that
     country you will have committed a trade mark infringement.
     A cautionary tale occurred to a high tech multi national
     US corporation in 1998 when they were using the Chinese
     version of their trademark in Taiwan. A local businessman had
     the benefit of this trademark in Taiwan. The US corporation
     had inadvertently overlooked this prior registration. The
     businessman took criminal proceedings for trademark
     infringement in the Taiwan courts and the US Corporation's
     Taiwan country manager was made a defendant to the action.
     At one stage the country manager was sentenced to six months'
     imprisonment which is a likely penalty for trademark
     infringement in Taiwan. The case has several hearings and
     appeals prior to it finally being resolved. Fortunately the
     sentence was not imposed as part of the final resolution.

3. Electronic Signatures

Most people are prepared to accept a hand written signature on
any document or letter without question. That is how it has been
done since time immemorial. Allowing for more that a few
celebrated forgers it has worked very well, in practice.

However over the new-fangled internet it is somehow different. In
any event people are being encouraged to use electronic
signatures. This is an electronic version of a signature, it can be
anything from typing your name at the bottom of an email to a
cryptographic set of data. It is used to identify the sender.

The system of secure electronic signatures has been agreed by the
EU and generally this is the system worldwide which is still in
its infancy.

The basis procedure is to have the electronic signature witnessed
by a third party. This is a dedicated witnessing company which is

called a Certification Service Provider (CSP) which gives a certificate (guarantee) to verify the signature.

This guarantee in practice cannot be open ended. There will almost always be some limitation on the liability. The certificate being subject to qualifications is called a "Qualified Certificate".

Therefore it is important if you intend to rely on an Electronic Signature that you find out the answer to two questions:

1. Duration – is the certificate still valid? Is it past its "sell by date"?

2. Is there any limit on its scope. For example, is there a financial limit of liability or a limit of the value of the transaction that it can support.

Electronic signatures are not in common use as yet however it is expected that more use will be made of this method of authentication.

4. Internet investigations

From time to time your company will see something on an internet site that it does not like. For instance, another company unlawfully selling your products or defamatory comments concerning your company.

It is the IT Professionals who will often be asked to conduct an investigation.

There are five things to bear in mind:

a) *The goal posts move.* What you see on an internet site one moment can be gone the next. It is essential that you capture the site content immediately in order to preserve the evidence in case it is changed and/or it is required in any court case or tribunal at a later date. This can be as easy as making a copy in Microsoft Word. However there are programs on the internet which can image the site in such a way as to preserve the entire site eg. webVCR which is inexpensive. There are programs which can reveal the history of the website and show pages for a specific day. This application would prove very useful in investigations. However if the evidence is to go before a court then it is best to keep it simple for the judge. Therefore evidence that you personally saw the web page on a particular day supported by a print out of the page made by you is by far the better evidence.

b) *Try to stop everybody in your company visiting the site.* Defamation or unlawful sale of products is a serious matter and will generate a lot of interest in your company. It is human nature for the employees be they managers, executives or lowly employees to see for themselves. This causes a great deal of unusual traffic on the suspect site and may alert the wrong doers to your investigation. Issuing a general notice for no one to go to the site, in my experience, is taken as an invitation for multiple visits. It is best to caution each person who is aware of the site to secrecy to allow your enquiry to proceed.

c) *Your own visit to the site may in some circumstances alert the owner* and therefore it is usually best if you use a non network computer to gather the information.

d) *Take down notices.* This is a notice requesting the Internet Service Provider (ISP) hosting the site to take it down. There is no magic in the format however where an ISP requires a certain form it is best to follow it. In the absence of any form from the ISP an email from you giving details of the problem e.g. defamatory comments will usually result in the offending item being removed very quickly. In the EU and the USA the ISP is not liable for content on it sites unless it becomes aware of it in which case it must, by law, act expeditiously to remove it. This is increasingly being interpreted as within 48 hours. Expect a very responsible attitude from the ISP. Even though they will not want to lose a customer they do not want to be sued either. They are running a business and a customer who is causing trouble for your business may be causing problems for other businesses. It is better that such a customer is identified. Often ISPs will have an abuse@ email link on their home page to assist you in making your complaint. In obvious cases the ISP will usually contact its customer and ask it to be taken down and that is usually the end of the matter. If there is doubt the ISP may decide to leave the offending item up although they do not normally wish to bear this risk.

e)   What if it is not possible to identify from an inspection of the site *who is responsible* for the offending content? ISPs are usually reluctant to provide the identity of the content owner. You can apply to the court for an order that the ISP reveal the identity. However you will probably need to bear the costs of this application unless the court can be convinced that the ISP has been unreasonable.

5.   Someone stole our name!

For instance, you do a search on Google® and you find that someone is using your name.

Here are the questions to ask:

1.   Is it in your industry?

2.   Are any of your customers deceived?

Someone is using your trademark on the Internet as his or her domain name.

Most domain names will be subject to the WIPO's (World Intellectual Property Organisation) Uniform Dispute Resolution Policy (UDRP). You can make a complaint and they will transfer the name to you if it is your mark or confusingly similar. The panel deciding will look to see if the user can show that they have some right in the name and if it is being used in bad faith. This is a cheap method of protecting your name. Sometimes it is better to approach the user of the domain and pay a fairly small sum to get your name back (as much as that may hurt).

Just because they are using your name does not guarantee you will get it back. If it is a borderline case you may need to go to court. Panels have decided that the so called xxxsucks name e.g. Microsoftsucks (which are fairly common websites usually set up by disgruntled former employees) are ok. Here the name is not confusing anybody. No one would think that they are dealing with Microsoft should they go to such a site.

6. Being spammed

As for the heavy duty industrial spammers if located and identified they can be stopped by an injunction under the civil law. A certain area in Miami has been identified as a haven for some industrial spammers. Microsoft has taken action against a number of allegedly large spammers. However the reality is that if the large spammers have not moved to a country out of reach of the laws of the western world then they will shortly do so. Therefore the solution to industrial spammers must lie with technical measures rather than the law.

From time to time your business will be targeted by UK or European companies touting their products or services. There is legislation to be introduced in the latter part of 2003 which provides that a person must "opt in" before receiving direct mail. That means that speculative mail shots like spam will be illegal. This is as a result of an EU Directive therefore all Europe countries will be implementing similar legislation.

However there are times when you will receive direct marketing from a UK company and will want it to stop. Usually this can be done by telling the company that you want to opt out. On the bottom of such emails there is a requirement to place information of however a person receiving the mail can opt out. If the spam persists then a threat to inform the Information Commissioner's Office will probably suffice. If the spam persists then make the complaint.

CHAPTER 10
OTHER LEGAL ISSUES

The 10 Most Frequently Asked Questions by IT Managers

Over the past three years there have been many legal questions from the 3,000 UK IT Managers who are steering their companies through the FAST Software Compliance Program. The questions have been answered by the FAST legal team being Julian Heathcote Hobbins, Senior Legal Counsel and Kameljit Sidhu, Investigator and myself. What follows, comes from that experience.

10 Most Frequently Asked Questions by IT Managers

1. Can I sell software once I have finished with it?

2. Can I keep backup copies?

3. Can I proceed with an action if the licence does not allow or disallow it?

4. What is the main point to check out in a software licence?

5. I can use the software for as long as I want, can't I?

6. How confidential is the confidentiality clause?

7. How can I ensure that the software meets the specification?

8. When can I say enough is enough and walk away from the contract?

9. I want to use this software but cannot find the developer or owner?

10. I have a software program installed but don't use it. Is that wrong?

This is an opportunity to use these questions to test your knowledge of IT law. I have given answers to each question in Appendix 2.

2. Outsourcing – what are the risks?

A decision to outsource requires time, planning and expense. However the idea of outsourcing often comes to the surface at a time of cost cutting and radical change that needs to be implemented yesterday.

The decision can be as quick as a few board presentations and a review of the numbers, and then solicitors are instructed to review the contract. The difficulties can be sorted out along the way. Management are always prepared to give this a go as they see the IT capability falling short ...."can it be any worse than it is now?".

Management are expecting the IT Professional to argue against change and therefore calls to slow down or think carefully are often devalued. However these calls need to be made in any event. The IT Professional can be the voice of reason. Here are two "slow down and let's think about this arguments":

• Gartner estimated that 50% of major outsourcing deals fail to achieve their business objectives and are terminated or need to be renegotiated. Litigation is a small step away.

• An outsourcing arrangement is usually a five year plus commitment rather than a short term fix. Therefore there is lots of time to regret any decision made in haste. If you keep in mind the sort of arrangement that the outsourcing service company would need to put in place to support your outsourcing needs, you will understand that this is a juggernaut and they will fight tooth and nail to ensure you stay the distance. It means that if you try and get out of the deal they will not hesitate to take you to court. There is too much money riding on this for them to do otherwise.

Here are six points that the IT Professional should bear in mind:

1. This is no time to save money but to find a lawyer who has done this before and be prepared to incur the legal costs of getting this right. There are lots of contract lawyers who will take on outsourcing projects. However if they have not had plenty of experience in the type of outsourcing deal that you are negotiating they may be using this as a learning experience. Ask what other experience they have had, speak to the IT managers in those companies and in other companies and see how it went. With 5 out of 10 going wrong this should be a great source of information.

2. The assets of the IT department may be sold to the outsourcing company. It is probably a bit late to suggest this but when making purchases by way of leasing or licensing then it would be prudent to ensure that these can be transferred in the event of outsourcing. Start making a list and identify those assets which are on lease or licence and ensure that these can be transferred to the outsourcing company. There are many asset management software tools to help you make inventories.

3. Software that you have purchased is normally on licence and you will need the consent of the software publisher to transfer these assets. This checking should be well in advance and preferably before you are committed to outsourcing. The consequences of not getting consent opens your company and you up to civil and criminal liability and therefore leaves you over a barrel in any negotiations with the software publisher. Software publishers have been known to "stiff" end users of software by charging a high fee or requiring the software to be repurchased. The outsourcing company may be able to help secure a speedy consent as they are often substantial customers of the software publisher.

4. The outsourcing company will want to ensure that you own any bespoke software or any that you have created in house. They will be concerned at using any software where they are unsure who owns it. Normally software created by your employees will belong to the company however where the software is created by a consultant it belongs to him if you have not stipulated in the contract with the consultant that it belongs to you (see *Copyright – the right to copy* at page 4 above).

5. The IT Professional should be involved with identifying the services required. A lot of the arguments are about services which were not anticipated by the agreement and need to be added on later. The contract should anticipate such changes.

6. In negotiations do not avoid the difficult issues. Deal with these head on. Otherwise they will rear up during the term of the contract.

3. Policies and Procedures

I cannot compete with the mountain of advice that IT professionals have on policies and procedures. Therefore I will focus on three main areas that I feel are important from a legal viewpoint:

1. Policies – get out of jail free?

Policies are not a "get out of jail free card". If the infringing software or other copyright work is on your network then the company is liable even if it did not know. However if you demonstrate that you have acted reasonably by having policies that were audited, updated and enforced it is likely to be evidence that you:

- Did not know or did not have reason to believe that the software had been copied say too many times. This would support your argument that you should not pay any damages. In effect it would make a software company reluctant to sue you since, if the court did not award damages, it may award costs against the software publisher for wasting court time.

- Did not know it was copied without permission. This would avoid criminal liability for the company and the manager if you can demonstrate that you did not know. The onus on the claimant in such cases is to prove knowledge beyond reasonable doubt. If this looks unlikely then no action will be commenced.

2. The importance of communicating policies and procedures to staff

It is important to have a documented system of communicating and continuing to communicate policies to staff. This is necessary to be seen to be doing the right thing to deter whistleblowers. If disciplinary proceedings are launched against staff and the company is taken to the Employment Tribunal then records may be necessary not only to prove the company records but also to demonstrate that the policies were communicated to staff and therefore the employee must have known the rules.

In tribunal or court proceedings it is best to anticipate a flat denial from the employee unless it can be proven in the form of written records.

3. How to communicate policies to staff

In the case of new employees these can be put in the employment contract. Otherwise a hard copy can be sent to the employee to sign and return. In the case of refusal to sign then that person should be denied access to sensitive data.

Depending on the size of the company it may be sufficient in large companies to send the policies electronically with an acknowledgement of receipt. Some companies have placed the policies on the login screen for one day and any employees logging in on that day clicked to acknowledge they have read the policies.

4. The terms of employees' contracts

It may be difficult to take disciplinary proceedings against an existing employee for contractual terms imposed after commencement of employment. The reason, as you know, is that the terms of the contract should be communicated at the time of the contract. To do so once the job has started may be too late (see *10 things to know about contract* at page 26 above).

This puts a question mark over attempts to change an employee's contract once he has started work. However it is an implied term that you can ask employees to change their working practices if it is right for the efficiency of the business. It is best to provide for a degree of flexibility in the contract of employment. Some companies have gone as far as getting existing employees to sign a new contract of employment giving some tangible benefit in return for example a one off extra day's holiday. If the company are complying with their legal obligations and the employee's refusal may be considered unreasonable, it is hoped that this may be seen as a too cautious approach and no inducement would be necessary. However each situation will depend on the facts and in changing an employee's contract of employment it is best to rely on legal advice.

5. Policies on Data Protection

There is no set way to communicate data protection policies to staff. It is likely that the Commissioner would require a company to take a reasonable approach to communicate its policies and procedures. What is reasonable will depend on the circumstances of each company. To involve a lawyer in deciding on that process would help to demonstrate to a court that the company were acting reasonably. A cheaper method would be to call the Commissioner's hotline and make a note of the advice.

You should keep a record to demonstrate that the company has included data protection in its training programs.

A comprehensive set of policies together with documented procedures which are regularly audited provide the legal protection required by IT Professionals.

PART 4
DEALING WITH THE EMERGENCIES

CHAPTER 11
LITIGATION, LITIGATION, LITIGATION

"the true object of war is peace" ancient Chinese proverb

Suing the pants off people

How do corporations decide to take civil proceedings? Is it a considered process? Or is it more likely to be more like this?

It is reported to the CEO that someone is ripping off the company product or name or taking liberties of some kind. **CEO goes into orbit.** Junior manager told to bring the head of the offender ASAP. He in turn goes to law firm and they get into court within 48 hours and obtain injunction. Junior manager is hero.

If the credits could roll at that point great – but often they don't. Defendants often do not lie down and die.

The IT Professional is often inadvertently drawn into the fray when the company decides to sue another company. No one expects the IT Professional to take the decision or be involved with the strategy however when appointing the blame for a botched legal dispute the IT Professional is a prime candidate. The IT Professional needs to protect the company and himself. It is not only that potential criticism but the amount of work that a hasty decision to sue can generate for the IT Professional and his team.

IT Professionals should not only be ready to do their part professionally but it may be useful to be aware of the pitfalls and the consequences of making the decision.

Here are 10 points for the IT Professional to be aware of:

1. *"Is litigation expensive"*.

    Well, to paraphrase Woody Allen "only if it is done right". How many minutes do you think you should spend before entering into an open-ended commitment to spend $'000's? The answer is "at least overnight".

2. *A caste iron witness is a rare thing.*

    In litigation the goal posts shift regularly. However reliable a witness appears to be there is usually some measure of disappointment. So shore up the evidence. Make sure you have copies of any computer-related evidence which is important for the action. Statements should be taken from any important witnesses to stop people changing their stories. Ask the lawyer to direct you in what evidence you need to gather.

3. *If you delay you may lose your right to get the court to grant emergency action such as raiding the opponents' offices or an emergency injunction.*

4. In a civil case the court are only going to allow your company the satisfaction of raiding the offender's premises in serious circumstances. However *there are orders that the court can make to obtain evidence*. These are less satisfying but cheaper.

5. *Involve lawyers at an early stage* otherwise the chance to get good evidence that will stand up in court may be lost. If the action is about IP then try and get a lawyer who works in that area. This is, probably, no time to do things on the cheap or use the CEO's brother in law.

6. *It is best not to bang the table in the lawyer's office.* This can spook some lawyers into issuing proceedings. Most lawyers spend their time keeping their clients out of court – hard to believe but true. However if the only way to keep the client happy is getting into court then it is very tempting for a lawyer to give the client what he wants. Fighting it to the company's last penny is not a problem for the lawyer.

7. *Litigation is time consuming and wearing*. It is a little bit like the army "hurry up and wait". The company must be prepared to do what it takes and allocate extra resources. If the company cannot stand the heat it is very embarrassing to step out of the kitchen half way through.

8. *An award of costs seldom covers legal bills*. All too often the defendant turns out not to be able to pay. A company should not enter litigation to make money. It is not a deal. The company will be lucky if it breaks even. It usually costs money.

9. *Injunctions come with a health warning* in the form of a cross undertaking in damages which all applicants must give in the event that an application is unsuccessful. Getting the injunction is the easy bit. Let's face it, injunctions are normally obtained when the other party is not even in court. It is when the matter returns to court after the satisfaction of the injunction being served that rocks start to be thrown back. Sometimes this is when your only witness is revealed as a drunken ex-con or having some other motives for his allegations.

10. *99% of cases settle sometimes at the court door*. So look for settlements and mediation at every turn. Leave your principles at the door: even for a large company sticking to them can have a high price tag. In IP matters the infringer may end up as your customer.

So why would anyone in their right mind enter into litigation? Well, touchy feely mediation is ok, however there are always people out there who want to rip you off. In IP for instance if your product is worth stealing then you will need to keep your finger on the trigger to deal with bandits. If you are not seen to be protecting your brand then being a soft touch is asking for trouble.

Being aware of the risks and knowing how to weald it makes litigation a valuable and effective weapon in business. In inexperienced hands it can be a fiasco.

Conducting Computer investigations

From time to time an employee will do something involving their computers in breach of the companies policies e.g, downloading pornography. Or for some other reason you will be required to examine the content of a computer.

As the IT Professional you must put on your investigator's hat. From a legal point of view this is all about how you go about gathering evidence to successfully sue someone later on or not be sued for being too ham-fisted in your investigations.

It is very easy to make a mess of such investigations. If it is an important issue then it is best for you to refuse point blank to conduct the investigation and instruct a forensic expert. How do you determine if it is an important issue? Is an employee likely to be dismissed? This type of investigation can be sensitive and end up in an employment tribunal? Could it be a police matter or could it end up in a civil court? If the answer to any of these questions is yes then you should not touch the computer and employ a forensic expert or contact the police immediately.

If you work for the type of company that would be reluctant pay for a forensic expert then here are more details of what can go wrong:

You will be ripped to pieces in court room cross examination.

Put yourself in a defence barrister's position. There is usually a strong case against his client otherwise the police would not have commenced the prosecution. He often has a client who can hardly string two words together and who is a positive liability if placed in the witness box. His best course is to challenge the evidence before the trial starts. If the evidence is thrown out then the case is dismissed without the defendant saying anything. If you were the barrister who would you pick on, the experienced police witnesses or the IT Professional who had never been trained in forensic evidence gathering who was trying to explain computers to a judge/jury. In this senario the IT Professional "is the weakest link". Barristers will know that the same tactic is worth trying in a civil court or an employment tribunal.

You will take the blame.

Every time the computer is booted up, the information on the computer changes. A modification to one file in this process can cause data to be lost from another file. The defence lawyer will argue that the computer evidence has been contaminated. He will say that it was all your fault as you know nothing about computer forensics and you visited the computer several times conducting ham-fisted investigations. Experts tend to make a copy of the hard disk and work on that preserving the original evidence.

It is far better to instruct an expert investigator to take the matter off your hands. However experts can be expensive as the hours mount up. A forensic inspection of a computer can take 15 hours or more. So remember that hourly rates can be deceptively cheap. It depends on how serious the matter is to your company and how hard you can argue with the Finance Manager that this is not a time to penny pinch.

Protecting your own software

With the increasing focus on CRM (Customer Relationship Management) systems businesses find that they have commissioned the design of software solutions which when tried and tested has value within their own industry. Some businesses successfully package and sell this software. I should note that in order to gain the benefit of this innovation the purchaser of the designed software must ensure that there is a complete assignment of the IPR in the software or a licence allowing the software to be transferred to others for payment.

So, congratulations, you are now the publisher of software and entitled to the profits of any purchase. However you have the obligation to fend off those bandits who want to rip you off. The Business Software Alliance (BSA) Survey in 2003 estimated that the price of 26% of software in business use remained unpaid. In a recent survey conducted by FAST end user IT managers responded that the use of unpaid for software in business could be as high as 50%. If this is the case, under-licensing is of epidemic proportions.

You should protect your investment by getting a licence drawn up by a lawyer and protecting your IPR by using non-disclosure and reseller agreements.

There are four main ways that you can get ripped off.

1. Under licensing

The main problem is under licensing.

Under licensing is a result of a customer buying a software product once, but copying it many times. Some end-users will understand that they are deliberately cheating – others copy the file without any thought. Copies of popular, easy-to-use products can spread like wild fire across a corporation.

Clearly continuing to use infringing copies of software in these circumstances, is a criminal offence. There is also personal criminal liability for the managers and directors of a company who turn a blind eye (see *Software infringement* at page 131 below). Companies infringing often quickly relented after the seriousness of the matter was pointed out to them and a settlement was conducted.

2. Incorporation of your software into another's product

A competitor is using your software. Sometimes this can be discovered at a trade fair, via an employee or consultant of the infringer blowing the whistle, or on receipt of an email advertising the product. There are three options:

- Take no action. Failing to defend IPR in this way seems to be a dangerous ploy and may cause difficulties for you when trying to protect your IPR in the future.

- The "with money" option is to sue the pants off them. If you have unlimited funds go for it. Your lawyer will launch injunction proceedings immediately, you can be in court in a matter of a day or two. The choice of the lawyer in this case is crucial. The easy part is getting the publisher to court and an order made. You need to consider each time if the drama of an urgent injunction can be justified in business terms. Sometimes focusing on testing the witness evidence together with the delay of gathering further evidence and then writing to the infringer gives a less satisfying but adequate and cheap result.

- The "without money" option is more humble but can be effective. You write a letter and hope that the infringer caves in. Police or Trading Standards are reluctant to take on these cases as they are usually complicated and they do not have the resources. However these are criminal offences and by continuing to sell another's product after being put on notice has risk for the company and its directors. In these circumstances letters pointing out the potential criminal liability to the executives and the board can be very effective. The customers of the company, once put on notice are in the same position. However caution needs to be exercised to ensure that the allegation can be proved. If you make an allegation and you cannot back it up with proof this can seriously backfire.

3. Resellers – carry on selling

Resellers who are terminated by you will sometimes continue to sell the product without passing any money on to you. Therefore choose your resellers carefully. If you part company ensure you serve an adequate notice of termination on the reseller. This lack of notice allows the reseller to say that he thought that he was allowed to continue (an implied licence). When caught, rogue resellers will sometimes just buy the product from your other resellers especially where you have lost control of your reseller channel. This is a criminal offence and should be reported to the police. Cases do need to be simply and comprehensively presented. A private prosecution is always a consideration.

4. Rogue employees and consultants

A frequent complaint from publishers centres round a consultant or employee stealing the source code. One small software publisher I know reported this happening on two occasions in two months. In the first instance a dismissed employee was found to have the source code in his bag. On the second occasion, the company was alerted when a consultant transferred the code out through the email system.

Hacked off – what can you do?

Increasingly businesses are concerned with the prospect of unauthorised access to their computer systems. There are no accurate statistics and a lot of businesses do not report such attacks. Most use a technical solution or an improvement in internal procedures to try and prevent any further hacking and then move on.

The law does address the issue of hacking in the Computer Misuse Act 1990. This has been a very unsuccessful piece of legislation in that few have tried to take advantage of it. However it will soon be amended so that it will become more user friendly. Basically it creates two basic offences:

1. *"Hacking"* with a penalty of 6 months imprisonment or fine. Where the hacking is linked with other crime the penalty can be up to 5 years imprisonment and unlimited fine.

2. *"Tampering"*. This means unauthorized modification of computer materials.

Often IT issues are not seen as important by the police. They are deterred by investigations which may lead into the unchartered waters of unfamiliar laws. The seriousness is difficult to demonstrate. They have many competing crimes to deal with and IT crimes take second place to wounding and fraud.

Specialist units set up by the police either deal only with the most serious computer related matters or are bogged down with paedophile investigations.

A private prosecution is a consideration.

Even if it is difficult to utilize the law hacking is a criminal offence and that in itself is a useful deterrent.

A LAWYER
ON YOUR TAIL

CHAPTER 12
NOT GETTING YOUR COMPANY SUED
AND KEEPING YOUR JOB

A lawyer on your tail?

A solicitor's letter

If a company has gone to the time and trouble of instructing a solicitor then this is a serious matter for your company and you should instruct a solicitor to advise you and reply on your behalf. To try and deal with a solicitor yourself often ends up making the matter worse for you.

A letter from an enforcement body

IP enforcement agencies like the Federation Against Software Theft ("FAST") and the Business Software Alliance (BSA) act on complaints received on their hotlines. As such complaints are often made by a business' own employees, it is ill advised for companies not to respond to the initial letter. But how do you respond? Say too much and you may give away valuable evidence. Say too little and you may prompt an escalation of the investigation against your company. If a company fails to respond this leaves the enforcement body with little choice but to consider civil or criminal action against your company and refer to the company's failure to reply on the question of costs.

In my experience few businesses do not respond.

But how to respond? It would be better if you handed this over to a lawyer so they could respond. But here are some key considerations:

1. Assuming, in the case of FAST or the BSA, that you are using software which you have not paid for and your object is to settle the matter. Settlement is a promise not to do it again and a payment of money to compensate the software publisher for the use. As you know this payment is by way of compensation and not punishment so the court would not order an outrageous sum of damages and the settlement will reflect this fact.

2. Read the letter and you will see that the nature of the complaint is set out in some detail. There are two types of letter. The first is where the body has evidence against your company (i.e. an investigation) and the other is an unsolicited request for information. If there is not sufficient detail in the letter for you to decide if this is an investigation or a request for information then a reply asking for clarification is in order. Again this should be done by a solicitor on your behalf.

3. Investigation

    Before an investigation letter is sent, it is usually the result of a detailed conversation and/or email exchange with the person giving the information. It should be obvious to you that if you are guilty then it is best to cooperate with such bodies without admitting liability and then move on.

4. What happens if you do not cooperate? The calculation that the enforcement body will make is whether they have enough evidence to take action. Commentary to the effect that enforcement bodies are not government agencies and they have no special powers is misleading. Enforcement bodies do not need special powers. They can use the existing law quite effectively. They can take civil proceedings against the company. This can include an application to the court to search premises. Courts do not grant such applications lightly, however where the defendant's reaction suggests that the evidence will be destroyed then a search order is appropriate. An injunction can be obtained to stop your company using

the software. However the main penalty in civil proceedings is probably the damage to the company's reputation and the cost. When IP is at issue and emergency legal procedures are utilized then the cost is very significant.

5. Where the unlawful use of software is in a business it is a criminal offence. This could prompt a private criminal prosecution against the company and its managers and directors if they have turned a blind eye to the unlawful use. Any person can take out their own private criminal prosecution against another person or company who is breaking the criminal law. However few use this right.

6. The other type of letter received from enforcement bodies is an unsolicited letter asking for information about your software licences. Can these just be thrown in the bin? That can work if they have no evidence against you. If you are feeling lucky you can try that approach. However it is necessary to appreciate there are different types of letter. Some software publishers retain a right in the licence for you to advise them of the number of copies in use. In that case it is a contractual duty of your company to reply to this letter. Having said that I have not seen a court case where a company were sued for failure to reply especially for a standard desktop application. The first letter is likely to be followed by a second letter.

7. Assuming that you are not a "throw them in the bin" person then you probably want to make some type of reply. It is not good to lie. If one of your employees has not shopped you to an enforcement body such letters have been known to prompt such a call.

8. The lawyer will almost certainly advise against any hasty response given by a busy IT Professional, which the company may regret later.

    Yet many IT Managers do not consult their legal department and scribble out a hasty reply. This for some can be like putting their neck in the noose.

It is like the story about a man in the French Revolution who was to be guillotined. Twice the guillotine failed to drop. The law was that if the guillotine failed to operate three times the condemned man was to be let free.

As he laid there, on the third time, looking up at the blade he said "Wait up, I think I can see the problem".

Giving out information when you are under no legal obligation to do so may not be such a shrewd move.

Software compliance as a defence

If you are raided or more frequently receive a letter from an enforcment body acting on behalf of a software publisher then it will be the conduct of the IT Professional which will be under the microscope.

When facing an audit by a software publisher you should bear in mind the following:

1. The software publisher will ask you for proof that you have a licence for the software. Although you are sure that you have such a licence, maybe due to a merger or because you have thrown it away, you may not be able to produce a copy of the licence. Increasingly software does not have a hard copy of a licence or some certificate of authenticty. The important thing to note is that a licence does not need to be a piece of paper. For instance, you have a right to residence in a country just because you lose your passport does not mean that you will be thrown out. You look for other ways that you can prove that you have a right to "residence".

2. The software publisher may expect you to be guided by its records. If you wish to rely on this method of software compliance then it is best to have your cheque book at the ready.

3. In an audit you will be expected to produce proof that you purchased the software:

    •   If you are a typical company it is unlikely that you have had a well established central purchasing procedure and your software licensing arrangements are probably in a mess. Often the IT Manager will say the software is locked down. However in my experience the legacy software prior to the date of the lockdown sustains unlicenced software. The IT Manager sits in front of this mess giving it a thin veneer of order until he is shopped often by one of his own IT staff. You will have a rough guess of how many software applications that the company is using. Laptops which are never audited could contain all sorts of unlawful software. You have probably thrown away boxes and other evidence and other computer media. The invoices to evidence purchase are held by the Accounts Department but are probably too brief and contain no reference numbers to identify a particular software application.

- If you have dealt with professional resellers over a long period then their records of sales to you may be the best supporting evidence. However most companies chop and change resellers. Some resellers are more disorganised that their customers. However some software publishers will not accept this and expect you to buy new software.

4. Can the software publisher insist on you buying new software? The software vendors remedies are to sue you for copyright infringement if you are using software without permission. If you carry on using the software after you are aware that you do not have permission then you can be guilty of a criminal offence. You are in a serious situation.

5. What can you do?

- The first thing to bear in mind – it is not for the software publisher to decide what is proof of purchase. Certainly the software publisher can sue you if it believes that you are using its software without a licence. However it is for the court to decide if you paid or not and it will take that decision after listening to you and considering all the circumstances.

- The first type of evidence that you can produce would be your explanation that the software was legitimately purchased. However this is not likely to be believed by the software publisher or the court without some supporting evidence. Other types of evidence would be a licence and or invoice with a reference number. A purchase order without any other supporting evidence is unlikely to be sufficient.

• As you are aware the onus is on the claimant to prove its case. However you may well be called upon to produce evidence of a licence by the court.

6. Software compliance

Many IT Managers are avoiding this situation by striving for software compliance.

The basic principles of Software Compliance are:

• Draw up policies and procedures

• Purchase a software audit tool

• Conduct an audit

• Continue to monitor software use.

If this approach is systematic then it is unlikely that an enforcement body will sue your company for software infringement. However the IT Professional must demonstrate a commitment to the principles of software compliance.

If an enforcement body proves that your company are using infringing software in your business then that is serious. However a software compliance procedure will help you to demonstrate that you the IT Professional did not connive (i.e. turn a blind eye). As you know the manager and director who turn a blind eye can personally be the subject of criminal proceedings. In civil proceedings for software infringement, a commitment to software compliance would be taken into account in any damages awarded and maybe on the question of costs.

One method of demonstrating a commitment is to join the FAST Software Compliance Program which addresses all these issues. For further details of this go to *www.fast.org*.

7. Connivance – Turning a blind eye

The most difficult job of the IT Professional may be to convince the Board of the legal implications of failing to managing a network efficiently. This is not only in respect of software compliance but also in respect of the obligations under the Data Protection Act and RIPA.

Each of these Acts makes it a criminal offence for the directors, managers, officers or controllers of the company not to comply.

I have set out the relevant sections in Appendix 3 in the hope that this may assist the IT Professional in making his argument for funding and resources.

4. Data Subject Access Requests

This is part of the Data Protection legislation. It allows any person to request a company to search its records for information. The idea behind this right is to stop companies keeping false or critical information about an individual without their knowledge. For instance, as bank or finance institution may have information to suggest that a person is a bad credit risk. Therefore any time that person asked for credit the request would be refused. The data subject access request would allow the person to request the information and if it is wrong to insist that it is corrected.

The data protection legislation provides that data should not be kept longer that is necessary. Therefore it allows an individual to check that a company is not holding prejudicial data concerning them long after the need has ceased.

Now that you understand the laudable reasons for the Data Subject Access Request procedure we can go on to the downside. It is a very powerful tool in the hands of an ex-employee or a person who is contemplating suing the company. A well known libel lawyer said that he would not be without it. If you want to be awkward with a company and cause it to waste time and money here is the option for you. Ironically, whereas the company can request £10 for dealing with the request the cost of doing so is expensive. A partner at a major law firm estimated the cost at £50,000 whereas a representative from the Information Commissioners Office suggested £200. It all depends how large the company is. However what we can say is that the administrative burden of properly dealing with these requests is onerous.

The best way to deal with a Data Subject Access Request is to ask the person what they want and hope that you can satisfy their exact request and bring the matter to an early conclusion. However as such requests usually come from people who have in one way or another fallen out with the company this may be a difficult option.

However some humble pie at the outset can result in substantial savings in terms of time and money.

For those of you for whom humility is not an option then here is what is in store in responding to a Data Subject Access Request:

1. You must search all your files – computer (including backup) and manual for references to the person. You are not expected to search every draw and therefore the concentration should be on databases and any organised manual filing system.

2. Once you have the information, hand over photocopies. Check these first to ensure that they do not refer to anyone else (as they have Data Protection rights too), if so blank out the names of anyone else.

3. Although handing over photocopies has become the norm if there is just too much paper to reasonably copy and hand over then a summary can be given.

4. You have 40 days to comply with the request. This time runs from the date of the *written* request however if you decide that you want to charge £10 for complying with the request then the time starts when the £10 is paid. There may be some people who do not want to pay £10 and a request for payment may bring the matter to a close. If the written request is not

clear then you can ask for clarification and time will not start until such clarification is received.

5. There are exceptions where the data is confidential such as conversations with your lawyer and security.

6. In practice, you will call up the Information Commissioner's Office to get advice. You will find the people at the office to be most helpful and reasonable. Often there is no firm answer but common sense is applied to decide if a certain document is to be handed over. I assume that in many cases the same Officer will be dealing with both parties in separate telephone conversations.

7. In the event that the requesting party is not satisfied that the company has complied then they can either apply to the court or report the matter to the Information Commissioner's Office. If you are dealing with "a crazy" this is good news for you and bad news for the Commissioner's Office. The Office will try to help resolve the matter in a reasonable manner. However if that is not possible then the Commissioner can issue an order for you to hand over certain information and if you do not comply criminal proceedings can be taken against the company.

8. You must also tell the person the reason for you keeping the information.

There are two methods of lessening the burden of Data Subject Access Requests. The first is to regularly cull unused data from your systems. In US companies this has been the practice for some years as there is an onerous duty to provide documents in any court hearing. The second is to have a good management and storage system. In some industries this more conservative approach is necessary when documents must be kept for lengthy periods of time.

Whistle Blowers

It is far more acceptable today for employees to tell, or rat, on their employers. In economic turndowns when companies are laying off employees calls to enforcement bodies such as FAST do increase. FAST receives about 1,000 calls on its Hotline each year.

This should be of concern to IT Professionals whose software and networks are in a mess.

However as you have seen employees do have a duty of confidentiality and therefore there is a limit on the type of information that employees can divulge about their employers businesses.

The Public Interest Disclosure Act 1998 ("the Whistle Blowers Act") was introduced to protect employees who decide to reveal their employers unethical practices. The Whistle Blowers Act protects employees who make a "Protected Disclosure" there are basically three requirements:

- The employee believes that their employer is committing a criminal offence or breach of civil law.

- The employee must believe the disclosure is "substantially" true, act in good faith and not make any personal gain. The Act has regard to the identity of the person to whom the disclosure is made.

- Was it reasonable in all the circumstances? For instance, could the employer have brought the matter to the attention of the company first without suffering detriment?

Employees sacked for blowing the whistle may have a claim in an Employment Tribunal where they may be awarded up to £50,000.

Information received from employees is often the best and most accurate information to support an action against the company.

Jaw, jaw not war, war – benefits of mediation

Mediation is otherwise called Alternative Dispute Resolution (ADR). It is all the rage in legal circles. Lawyers are qualifying as mediators in increasing numbers. Courts are referring matters to mediation as part of the court procedure.

Mediation is a very simple concept. The mediator is the boy in the playground who intervenes to stop two other boys fighting. Hopefully the two boys see sense and walk off and the matter is solved. In mediation the two parties in dispute agree to meet with a mediator (usually a lawyer) to work out their differences rather than battling it out in the courts. As about 99% of cases settle before they go to court, often at the court doors then mediation seems a perfect solution.

In practice, mediation has been less popular with business than was expected. It is easy to see the sense in sorting out other peoples' problems in this way but more difficult to work out your own problems. Often too much water has gone under the bridge for any compromise to be reached.

For years, lawyers have been advising against litigation as it can be a very time consuming, emotionally draining and expensive experience. However clients normally hope that the other side will see sense and give in. It is only after months or years that both parties have had enough and settle.

The thing to know about mediation is that it does not feel in the short term a win/win situation. Both parties may leave it feeling that they have lost face and money. However a quick solution to a dispute, however painful in my experience, is very cost effective.

The mechanics of a typical mediation are as follows. All parties gather in one neutral office. Sometimes the opposing parties will be camped in different rooms. There are no formal rules. Lawyers can be in attendance too. The mediator will flit from room to room trying to establish the issues. As the day proceeds the mediator will try and assess the bottom line of each of the parties. As the afternoon or evening progresses the parties will or will not be enticed by the idea of resolving the situation there and then.

Most mediators will say that it does not matter which industry is the subject of the mediation. However in my experience parties do prefer a mediator who can understand their industry. In order to find a mediator. There is a central organisation dealing with mediation *www.cedr.co.uk*. There are also lists of mediators with various trade bodies. FAST has a mediation panel consisting of lawyers who have knowledge of the software and IT industry (see *www.fast.org*).

Mediation may not be the solution to all disputes but it is always worth considering as a comparatively cost and time effective (if slightly wimpish) solution.

INTERNATIONAL IT
PROFESSIONALS
OF SLOUGH

CHAPTER 13
THE INTERNATIONAL IT PROFESSIONAL

As you are aware *Law for IT Professionals* was intended to give the bottom line.

However to further complicate the IT Professional's lot he is often called upon to deal with the legal or regulatory systems of other countries. In international terms he is not facing just a mountain of information but a whole mountain *range* of information. He can ignore the issues and risk being broad sided which is not really the preferred option for the International IT Professional. Alternatively he can try and get a grasp of the laws of other countries to avoid the pitfalls.

I have practised as a solicitor and a barrister in the UK, as a solicitor in Hong Kong and Australia. I worked for two years in one of Canada's top law firms. In each country I worked in many different legal areas.

I must confess that I didn't really see much difference in the law between all those countries. I don't wish to be branded as a heretic but it all looked pretty much the same to me.

If I am right then that is a real boon for the International IT Professional as he can learn the bottom line of the law in one country and apply it across the board. He can have a good idea of the problem areas whatever his geographic responsibilities. He can sound great in that job interview for the Singapore post (with maid and swimming pool).

Too good to be true? Let me explain further:

1. Whatever countries you are in the basic legal problems do not change. For the most part the twenty areas of law concerning

IT Professionals in all countries are licensing, pornography, data protection, employee monitoring (in the UK-RIPA), confidentiality agreements, restrictive covenants, outsourcing, mergers and acquisitions, litigation, policies, internet investigations, directors' liability, copyright, vicarious liability, defamation, human rights, regulations on selling over the internet (in the UK-distance selling), web sites, electronic signatures and contract (in particular computer services contracts).

2. History is on the side of the English-speaking International IT Professional. The British Empire, which included so many countries, left the legacy of the English legal system. This means that all the commonwealth countries and even the USA share the same legal root called the "common law" system. You will recall from television that the US legal terminology sounds so familiar. This is not only true for the countries in which I worked (Australia, Hong Kong, Canada, England) but also applies to New Zealand, Malaysia, Singapore, India, Sri Lanka etc.

3. More than that, in an increasingly global economy industries are calling for all countries to apply best practice in the law, so one country will model its new laws on the best practice of laws in other countries or at least take the laws of other countries into account. Especially when dealing with technical or "new fangled" issues such as the issues faced by International IT Professionals. For instance Data Protection legislation is very similar in most countries that have implemented it (apologies if you find this depressing).

4. Some laws such as copyright are developed by international treaty so they are very similar. The European Union is endeavouring to harmonise the laws of member states (although this has got a long way to go).

5. So how confident can you be when dealing with countries whose laws are not based on the English common law. The answer is: not very confident. So do not make any major assumptions in these countries.

6.   Having said that I have been involved with the law in some of those "other" countries such as the PRC, Taiwan, Japan, Korea and Indonesia. There were familiar aspects to the law. So there is room for gut feel. In some cases the procedures adopted were radically different but in my view a whole lot better.

So to a certain extent law cuts across international barriers.

Therefore a greater similarity of law being imposed by globalised industry and increasing awareness by government of best practice from country to country is good news for the International IT Professional.

So why do individual lawyers seem unwilling to give the general international advice that the IT professional increasingly requires?

There are two reasons:

1)   Understandably lawyers (except maybe IP lawyers) have traditionally been unwilling to offer a view of the law of other countries as they must get it right – a good guess may be enough for the IT Professional but falls short of the standard expected of lawyers by their insurers.

2)   Lawyers have become increasingly more specialised as legislation has become more complex. The lawyer must get it right so it is easier to call in a colleague to advise on his area of expertise.

The downside of this approach is that two lawyers are working on your matter rather than one. A seasoned IT/IP lawyer can be the general practitioner that you require. So choose carefully. The list of IT/IP lawyers at *www.fast.org* is a good starting point.

Note: To support the International IT Professional my publishers and I will be collaborating on a series of supplements on the laws of certain countries. These will be offered for download in an easily readable format.

These supplements will give the bottom line of the laws in other Commonwealth and "common law" countries. They are intended to be readable and brief.

MORE ABOUT FAST

The Federation Against Software Theft (FAST) became the world's first software copyright organisation when it was set up by the British Computing Society's Copyright Committee in 1984. Its aim was to lobby Parliament for changes in the Copyright Act of 1956. The Act was re-written and is now the Copyright Designs & Patents Act, 1988.

FAST has been responsible for bringing about changes in the law, in step with trends in computer and software crime, and has brought many software thieves to court. FAST continues to lobby for improvements to current legislation covering copyright, working in tandem with similar bodies internationally.

Today FAST protects software manufacturers' copyright through the prosecution of software fraud. Within its industry membership programme, FAST works alongside many major software publishers and distributors, hardware manufacturers and law firms.

FAST has also taken on a broader remit in the areas of education and enforcement, promoting the effective and legal use of software and helping organisations to maximise their software and hardware investments. The FAST Corporate Membership programme is arguably the most successful software user education programme available anywhere in the world. The programme, which has made software theft a boardroom issue, ensures that information, training and support are available to help organisations of all sizes understand software licensing and control their software assets. FAST Corporate Membership is now recognised as an essential step on the path to a legal software environment.

FAST Corporate Services Limited
Clivemont House, 54 Clivemont Road, Maidenhead, Berks SL6 7BZ
www.fast.org.uk

APPENDIX 1
EXAMPLE END USER LICENCE

This licence is the copyright of FAEGRE BENSON HOBSON AUDLEY LLP, solicitors and kindly supplied by their partner Robert Bond.

Read..........

WARNING!!

WE OWN THE COPYRIGHT TRADEMARK, TRADE NAMES, PATENTS AND OTHER INTELLECTUAL PROPERTY RIGHTS SUBSISTING IN OR USED IN CONNECTION WITH THE ENCLOSED SOFTWARE INCLUDING ALL DOCUMENTATION AND MANUALS AND ALL OTHER COPIES WHICH YOU ARE AUTHORISED TO MAKE BY THIS AGREEMENT ('THE SOFTWARE'). IT IS UNLAWFUL TO LOAD THE SOFTWARE INTO A COMPUTER WITHOUT OUR LICENCE. WE ARE WILLING TO LICENSE THE SOFTWARE TO YOU ONLY ON THE CONDITION THAT YOU ACCEPT ALL THE TERMS CONTAINED IN THIS LICENCE AGREEMENT AND RETURN THE SOFTWARE LICENCE REGISTRATION CARD TO US AT THE SPECIFIED ADDRESS WITHIN 14 DAYS OF PURCHASE OF THE SOFTWARE. PLEASE READ THIS LICENCE AGREEMENT CAREFULLY BEFORE BREAKING THE SEAL ON THE DISK ENVELOPE. BY OPENING THIS PACKAGING YOU AGREE TO BE BOUND BY THE TERMS OF THIS AGREEMENT. IF YOU DO NOT AGREE WITH THESE TERMS AND CONDITIONS WE ARE UNWILLING TO LICENSE THE SOFTWARE TO YOU, AND YOU SHOULD NOT OPEN THIS DISK PACKAGE. IN SUCH CASE YOU SHOULD, WITHIN 14 DAYS OF PURCHASE, RETURN THE UNOPENED DISK PACKAGE AND ALL ACCOMPANYING ITEMS TO US OR YOUR SUPPLIER WITH PROOF OF PURCHASE FOR A FULL REFUND.

1. LICENCE

    In consideration of your agreement to the terms of this Agreement, we grant you (the individual or entity whose name and address appears on the Registration Card) a perpetual, non-exclusive right to use the Software in accordance with **Clause 2** below. This licence is personal to you as the purchaser of the Software and the licence granted herein is for your benefit only.

2. PERMITTED USE

As purchaser of the authorised copy of the Software, you may, subject to the following conditions:

2.1 load the Software into and use it on a single computer (of the type identified on the package) which is under your control;

2.2 copy the Software for backup and archival purposes and make up to two copies of the documentation (if any) accompanying the Software, provided that the original and each copy is kept in your possession and that your installation and use of the Software does not exceed that allowed by this Agreement;

2.3 transfer the Software, on a permanent basis only, to another person by transferring all copies of the Software to that person and/or destroying copies not transferred. The other person must agree to the terms of this Agreement and on such a permanent transfer, the licence of the Software to you will automatically terminate.

3. RESTRICTIONS ON USE

You may not nor permit others to:

3.1 load the Software into two or more computers at the same time. If you wish to transfer the Software from one computer to another, you must erase the Software from the first hard drive before you install it onto a second hard drive;

3.2 sub-license, assign, rent, lease or transfer the licence or the Software or make or distribute copies of the Software except as permitted by this Agreement;

3.3 translate, reverse engineer, decompile, disassemble, modify or create derivative works based on the Software except as permitted by law;

3.4 make copies of the Software, in whole or part, except for backup or archival purposes as permitted hereunder;

3.5 use any backup copy of the Software for any purpose other than to replace the original copy in the event that it is destroyed or becomes defective;

3.6 copy the written materials (except as provided by this Agreement) accompanying the Software;

3.7 adapt, modify, delete or translate the written material accompanying the Software in any way for any purpose whatsoever;

3.8 vary, delete or obscure any notices of proprietary rights or any product identification or restrictions on or in the Software.

4. UNDERTAKINGS

You undertake to:–

4.1 ensure that, prior to use of the Software by your employees or agents, all such parties are notified of this licence and the terms of this Agreement;

4.2 reproduce and include our copyright notice (or such other party's copyright notice as specified on the Software) on all and any copies of the Software, including any partial copies of the Software;

4.3 hold all drawings, specifications, data (including object and source codes), software listings and all other information relating to the Software confidential and not at any time, during this licence or after it's expiry, disclose the same, whether directly or indirectly, to any third party without our consent.

5. TITLE

As licensee you own only the diskette or medium on which the Software is recorded or fixed. You may retain the media on termination of this Agreement provided the Software is erased. We shall at all times retain ownership of the Software.

6. WARRANTY

6.1 Subject to **Clause 6.2**, we warrant that for a period of 90 days from the date of your purchase of the Software ('the Warranty Period'):

6.1.1 the medium on which the Software is recorded will be free from defects in materials and workmanship under normal use. If the diskette fails to conform to this warranty, you may, as your sole and exclusive remedy, obtain (at our option) either a replacement free of charge or a full refund if you return the defective diskette to us or to your supplier during the Warranty Period with a dated proof of purchase;

6.1.2 the copy of the Software in this package will materially conform to the documentation that accompanies the Software. If the Software fails to operate in accordance with this warranty, you may, as your sole and exclusive remedy, return all of the Software and the documentation to us or to your supplier during the Warranty Period, along with dated proof of purchase, specifying the problem, and we will provide you either with a new version of the Software or a full refund (at our option).

6.2 We shall not be liable under the warranties given in **Clause 6.1** above if the diskette or the Software fails to operate in accordance with the said warranty as a result of any modification, variation, or addition to the Software not performed by us or caused by any abuse, corruption or incorrect use of the diskette or Software, including use of the Software with equipment or other software which is incompatible.

7. DISCLAIMER

We do not warrant that this Software will meet your requirements or that its operation will be uninterrupted or error free. We exclude and hereby expressly disclaim all express and implied warranties or conditions not stated herein (including without limitation, loss of profits, loss or corruption of data, business interruption or loss of contracts), so far as such exclusion or disclaimer is permitted under the applicable law. THIS AGREEMENT DOES NOT AFFECT YOUR STATUTORY RIGHTS.

8. LIABILITY

8.1 Our liability to you for any losses shall not exceed the amount you originally paid for the Software.

8.2 In no event will we be liable to you for any indirect or consequential damages even if we have been advised of the possibility of such damages. In particular, we accept no liability for any programs or data made or stored with the Software nor for the costs of recovering or replacing such programs or data.

8.3 Nothing in this Agreement limits liability for fraudulent misrepresentation or our liability to you in the event of death or personal injury resulting from our negligence.

8.4 You hereby acknowledge and agree that the limitations contained in this Clause are reasonable in light of all the circumstances.

9. TERMINATION

9.1 The Agreement and the licence hereby granted to use the Software automati-cally terminates if you:

9.1.1 fail to comply with any provisions of this Agreement;

9.1.2 destroy the copies of the Software in your possession;

9.1.3 voluntarily return the Software to us.

9.2 In the event of termination in accordance with **Clause 9.1** you must destroy or delete all copies of the Software from all storage media in your control.

10. SEVERABILITY

In the event that any provision of this Agreement is declared by any judicial or other competent authority to be void, voidable, illegal or otherwise unenforceable or indications of the same are received by either you or us from any relevant competent authority, we shall amend that provision in such reasonable manner as achieves the intention of the parties without illegality or, at our discretion, such provision may be severed from this Agreement and the remaining provisions of this Agreement shall remain in full force and effect.

11. ENTIRE AGREEMENT

You have read and understand this Agreement and agree that it constitutes the complete and exclusive statement of the Agreement between us with respect to the subject matter hereof and supersedes all proposals, representations, understandings and prior agreements, whether oral or written, and all other communications between us relating thereto.

12. ASSIGNMENT

This Agreement is personal to you and you may not assign, transfer, sub-contract or otherwise part with this Agreement or any right or obligation under it without our prior written consent.

13. WAIVER

Failure or neglect by either party to exercise any of its rights or remedies under this Agreement will not be construed as a waiver of that party's rights nor in any way affect the validity of the whole or part of this licence nor prejudice that party's right to take subsequent action.

14. LAW AND DISPUTES

This Agreement and all matters arising from it are governed by and construed in accordance with the laws of England and Wales whose courts shall have exclusive jurisdiction over all disputes arising in connection with this Agreement and the place of performance of this Agreement is agreed by you to be England.

If you have any questions about this Agreement, write to us at [   ] or call us at [   ].

SOFTWARE LICENCE REGISTRATION CARD

I have read and fully understand and agree to be bound by and comply with the Agreement, a copy of which is printed overleaf.

Signed by [   ]

Dated [   ]

Printed Name [   ]

Title [   ]

On behalf of [   ]
Company [   ]
Address [   ]

APPENDIX 2
10 MOST FREQUENTLY ASKED QUESTIONS

The 10 questions below are the 10 Most Frequently Asked Questions by IT Managers. Here are the answers. How did you do? If you scored less than 5 start reading the book again. If you scored less than 2 become a plumber.

1. Can I sell software once I have finished with it?

The answer is it all depends if the licence permits it. So buying second hand software from an auction site where you are given possession of the original disk seems legitimate. However have a look at the conditions of the click wrap license and you may find you have not bought the right to use it.

2. Can I keep backup copies?

Yes. You can keep back up copies? The question is how many copies are you allowed to keep and in what circumstances? This in effect is usually the disk on which the software is purchased. If you have a system where you keep a further backup in a secure location as part of your recovery plan you can keep another. There may be other reasons that you can argue to keep further copies. However pirates caught with software being copied onto recordable CD's will often claim that it was a back up copy. So claims that backups are being kept for lawful reasons are treated with some suspicion.

Note: you can also decompile or reverse engineer the software to find out how it can interface with another program.

3. Can I proceed with an action if the licence does not allow or disallow it?

You want to use the software in a particular way however you look at the licence and it does not say you cannot use it in that manner but does not say that you can. A licence is a permission. If it does not say expressly you can do a certain act then you cannot do it. You can always approach the software publisher and request permission. It is hoped that all publisher would allow uses which were inconveniencing their customers and not affecting the value of the software.

4. What is the main point to check out in a software licence?

There are quite a few points to check such as ensuring you get the right type of licence for your company. However the main point is, in my view, to ensure that the licence is granting the rights to the correct company. In your group you may have several limited companies. If the licence reads that it is granted to X Limited then it may not extend to other companies in the group e.g. X Holdings Limited. So ensure that the licence is as wide as possible to cover all the companies and people who need to use the software. Fail to do so and you may find the software publisher wishing to charge for any extension later on. For example any consultants who you wish to use the software.

(see *Types of licence* at page 73 above).

5. I can use the software for as long as I want, can't I?

When you buy software you may think it will last forever and you can sell it on. However the licence may say it is only for a limited period e.g. an annual licence fee. In some cases this is understandable such as anti-virus software which requires daily updates. However it is fairly common to find some time limitation which may not be supported by any logic. When reading the licence look for words such as perpetual or irrevocable which mean it is tantamount to owning it. Consider negotiating anything less. Try to make it your decision to get an upgrade not a decision forced upon you. (See *Negotiating a Software Contract* at page 90.)

6. How confidential is the confidentiality clause?

From time to time in business you may be asked to sign a confidentiality clause or agreement. It may be for someone selling an idea, or who hasn't brought a product to market but wishes to give you a preview.

Although this is understandable make sure this is not so limiting as to disrupt your usual business practices. The law will enforce such agreements. If you have been told a trade secret or some other confidential information then you are expected not reveal such information.

In fact the law does not require any document at all. However without a document it is difficult to establish what information was confidential and what information was handed over (see *Confidentiality agreements* at page 65 above).

7. How can the law help ensure that the software meets the specification?

Software is notorious for having bugs and buyers expect problems. However there should be a promise by the software seller that the software works in accordance with specifications. Such promises are called "warranties". If you are negotiating a licence of a software application, look out for this warranty and try to delete words that limit the promise. (See *Negotiating a Software Contract* at page 91.)

8. When can you say enough is enough and walk away from the contract?

It is a little like getting married at the time of the reception no one gives any thought to the possibility of a divorce or even serious disagreement. However like marriage entering into a software agreement can be full of contention.

If the relationship really terms sour you may want to walk away. However the way the law views it is you made the deal however bad it is. The service or the product has got to be really bad before you can get out of it. If you walk away you may find yourself being sued by the supplier for the money you promised. He may be able to show that you were under a contract and had to stick to your word however bad his behaviour has been. The bottom line is before walking away get a lawyer's advice: that will probably be cautious. Try to document the case against the supplier by writing to him to say what is wrong.

This is where the terms warranties and conditions come in. There are certain terms of the contract that the supplier must provide these are "conditions" and if he breaches the conditions you can walk away. Then there are terms called "warranties" and here you must stay with the contract and the supplier can compensate you in damages (see *Software Contracts – what happens if it all goes wrong* at page 87 above).

9. I want to use this software but cannot find the developer or owner?

Then if you use it without permission it would be a copyright infringement under the civil law.

Could it be a criminal offence? I do not know of any prosecutions in these circumstances. It would probably be best not to use if. It may be possible to argue it was abandoned and there was no dishonesty intended. However those are arguments which are more suitable to the laws relating to theft rather than copyright. I doubt if any criminal action would be taken in these circumstances provided it was a genuine belief and enquires to find the owner had been made.

If you need to find the owner of the software even if a company has gone bust or person made bankrupt there is often someone appointed by the court to deal with the affairs of the company or person. Usually a liquidator or administrator. A search of a government register (e.g. Companies Register at Companies House) can be made to locate the correct person.

10. I have a software program installed but don't use it. Is that wrong?

Every time you boot up your system the software is technically in use. The law says that if software is in use (even in this limited capacity) you must have a licence for that software. So it is best to uninstall programs.

A problem for IT Professionals managing a system is that there are many .exe files on the network which have built up over the years. These .exe programs which are small fragments of entire applications are considered software and should therefore be covered by a licence.

What about where you store a computer and you do not turn it on? This assumes when you loaded (copied) the program onto your computer you had a licence to use it then for some reason the licence expired or you used it for a copy on another computer. If you are not using the computer it is not being copied. This may be a sufficient argument for a consumer. However the criminal law allows for an offence of being in possession of software in the course of business without a licence to use it.

All in all it is best to uninstall programs where you have not got a licence.

APPENDIX 3
KEY LEGISLATION

Copyright Designs and Patent Act 1988

Section 110 (1) – Offences by body corporate: liability of officers

Where an offence under s.107 committed by a body corporate is proved to have been committed with the consent or connivance of a director, manager, secretary, or similar officer of the body, or a person purporting to act in any such capacity, he as well as the body corporate is guilty of an offence and liable to be proceeded against and punished accordingly.

Note: s.107 refers to copyright infringement.

Data Protection Act 1998

Section 61(1) – liability of directors etc.;

Where an offence under this Act has been committed by a body corporate and is proved to have been committed with the consent or connivance of or to be attributable to any neglect on the part of any director, manager, secretary or similar officer of the body corporate or any person who was purporting to act in any such capacity, he as well as the body corporate shall be guilty of that offence and be liable to be proceeded against and punished accordingly.

Regulation of Investigatory Powers Act 2000 (RIPA)

Section 79(1) – criminal liability of directors etc.;

Where an offence under any provision of this Act other than a provision of Part III is committed by a body corporate and is proved to have been committed with the consent or connivance of, or to be attributable to any neglect on the part of–

(a) a director, manager, secretary or other similar officer of the body corporate, or

(b) any person who was purporting to act in any such capacity,

he (as well as the body corporate) shall be guilty of that offence and liable to be proceeded against and punished accordingly.

BIBLIOGRAPHY

1. *Law and the Internet: a Framework for Electronic Commerce*
   Lillian Edwards and Charlotte Welde;

   Email, the Internet and the Law
   Tim Kevan and Paul McGrath

2. *Data Protection in the UK*
   Peter Carey;

   Data Protection Law
   David Bainbridge

3. *Copinger and Skone James on Copyright*
   Kevin Garnett Johnathan Rayner James and Gillian Davies

4. *Archbold Criminal Pleadings Evidence and Practice*
   Editor Richardson

5. *Cheshire Fifoot & Fumstons Law of Contract*

6. *Software Copyright Law*
   David Bainbridge;

   Software Licensing
   David Bainbridge

7. *Intellectual Property*
   David Bainbridge

8. *Blackstones Statutes on Intellectual Property Law*
   Andrew Christie & Stephen Gare

9. *Equity*
   Robert Bond

10. *Electronic Business Law*
    Lexis Nexis Butterworths

INDEX

Other EMIS Professional Publishing Products

EMIS Professional Publishing provides a wide range of published materials in this area. For newsletters and law reports, you can request a free sample. To order or for more details, see our website *www.emispp.com*.

Intellectual Property and Information Technology Law

David Bainbridge BSc, LLB, PhD, CEng, MICE, MBCS, Reader in Law, University of Aston

Intellectual Property and Information Technology Law presents articles on key developments in each of the major areas of Intellectual Property: *Trade Marks *Copyright *Patents *Designs *Licensing and *Computer Software. Essential developments in intellectual property law and procedure in the UK, Europe and worldwide are covered in an accessible and concise way. In-depth articles also cover issues of particular concern.

A4 Newsletter and single user licence for electronic service
2003 price £150.

The EMIS E-Law Service

This new paper and email service provides readers with a monthly summary of the key developments in e-commerce, telecommunications and mobile technology – which together can be termed digital or "e" media. Practical and well written the articles come from leading firms of solicitors.

2003 Price £200

Legal Protection of Software

Richard Morgan, Consultant, Cornwell Affiliates **and** Kit Burden, Partner, Barlow Lyde & Gilbert

This book is a practical and readable text, full of checklists and precedent provisions so as to leave the reader with a complete roadmap through the complex provisions of intellectual property law as it applies to the software industry.

£38   ISBN 1 85811 294 X

Data Protection Law

David Bainbridge BSc, LLB, PhD, CEng, MICE, MBCS, Reader in Law, University of Aston

Far more than just annotated legislation, this 400page text is full of checklists, flowcharts and other tools, rendering it invaluable to advisers and data users alike.

£36.00   ISBN 1 85811 203 6

IP and IT Databases

David Bainbridge BSc, LLB, PhD, CEng, MICE, MBCS, Reader in Law, University of Aston

Having access to the right information at the right time is crucial in intellectual property and information technology law. These databases offer pertinent summary and comment on key law.

2002 Service £75+VAT (£88.13) STUDENT PRICE ON APPLICATION

Software Licensing, Second Edition

David Bainbridge BSc, LLB, PhD, CEng, MICE, MBCS, Reader in Law, University of Aston

Of the first edition: "Strongly recommended" Computer Law. "Highly readable, full of help and advice." Computing. David Bainbridge provides expert advice and guidance on the drafting of licence agreements. The emphasis is on how licensing agreements work in practice, how they are negotiated and what occurs in the event of dispute.

£42.00   1 85811 191 9

E-mail, the Internet and The Law

Tim Kevan BA (Cantab) Barrister, 1 Temple Gardens; Paul McGrath Barrister, 1 Temple Gardens

The internet and email is at the heart of the modern world's communications. This volume will be essential for all companies wishing to set and maintain internal policies, as well as all companies trading on the internet.

£28.00   ISBN 1 85811 268 0

Valuation and Exploitation of Intellectual Property

John Sykes Solicitor, Partner, Lupton Fawcett; Kelvin King, Valuation Consulting

When a company buys another company, how does it value its brands? When an investor is assessing the value of a technology business how does it value its assets? This book takes the reader through the legal and accounting principles that govern the valuation of IP assets.

£95.00 Hardback 1 85811 281 8

BUY ANY TITLE ON OUR WEBSITE AT *WWW.EMISPP.COM*

EMIS Professional Publishing, 31-33 Stonehills House, Welwyn Garden City, AL8 6PU
Tel: 01707 334823   Fax: 01707 335022   DX 144000 Welwyn Garden City 5